Anti-Badiou

Anti-Badiou

On the Introduction of Maoism into Philosophy

François Laruelle

Translated by *Robin Mackay*

BLOOMSBURY

LONDON • NEW DELHI • NEW YORK • SYDNEY

Bloomsbury Academic

An imprint of Bloomsbury Publishing Plc

50 Bedford Square	175 Fifth Avenue
London	New York
WC1B 3DP	NY 10010
UK	USA

www.bloomsbury.com

Originally published in French as *Anti-Badiou: Sur l'introduction du maoïsme dans la philosophie* © Éditions Kimé, 2011

This English translation © Bloomsbury Publishing Plc, 2013

British Library Cataloguing-in-Publication Data

A catalogue record for this book is available from the British Library.

ISBN: HB: 978-1-4411-9574-6

Library of Congress Cataloging-in-Publication Data

Laruelle, François.

Anti-Badiou: on the introduction of Maoism into philosophy / François Laruelle; translated by Robin Mackay. First [edition]. pages cm

Includes bibliographical references and index.

ISBN 978-1-4411-9574-6 (hardcover) – ISBN 978-1-4411-5870-3 (epub) – ISBN 978-1-4411-9076-5 (ebook (pdf)) 1. Badiou, Alain–Criticism and interpretation. 2. Badiou, Alain–Political and social views. 3. Communism. 4. Philosophy, French–20th century. I. Mackay, Robin (Philosopher), translator. II. Title.

B2430.B274.L3713 2013

194–dc23

2012021338

Typeset by Fakenham Prepress Solutions, Fakenham, Norfolk NR21 8NN

Printed and bound in India

Contents

Abbreviations

FP	Forces of Production
K	Kant
F	Fichte
NP	Non-Philosophy
OV	Ontology of the Void
PSM	Principle of Sufficient Mathematics
PSP	Principle of Sufficient Philosophy
RP	Relations of Production

Preface

Re-educating philosophy through mathematics: Purification and terror

Why Badiou? He represents the introduction of Maoism into philosophy, as undertaken by a "great" philosopher—that is to say, a philosopher entirely apart—with all the inherent risk of this will and this greatness. He is an apogee of the modern tradition of philosophy, of its very essence brandished like a standard in the face of mathematics and with its aid. But, beneath this objective appearance, other stakes can be discerned. It would render Badiou banal to describe him merely as a master of "Western" modernity. His project is more profound: his intention is to "re-educate" philosophy. Beyond the various proclamations and summations—which we shall not rely on to prove our point at the level of the most obvious principles—he pursues *the project of the re-education of philosophy through mathematics, and not at all that of the constitution of a mathematically based science of philosophy (supposing such a thing were possible)*. This enterprise has no equivalent in the history of philosophy (except perhaps

Plato); but it does have a political model, in the recent history of communism. Badiou would have it that "modernity" is a fusion of Platonist mathematicism and Maoism, thus demonstrating his astonishing plasticity, his ability to fuse with liberalism on one hand, mathematicism on the other. From this point of view, mathematicism is the condition of communism, with the authoritarian Platonist model finding a new lease of life in Maoism.

Although at first glance the characteristically conservative aspect of all philosophy prevails in Badiou, in fact he cedes nothing to the dominant tradition of philosophy, above all "continental" and "modern" philosophy. He practices mathematics to teach and to teach himself, at best to illustrate the concept; a matter of apprenticeship, of the deciphering of a constituted science about which and through which philosophy can educate itself. But to the best of our knowledge, it is not a matter of actual mathematical production, as in Plato and a few rare so-called "modern" classics. Here, the philosopher of mathematics remains a philosopher, and not a mathematician. That is to say that, if there is no chance here of producing a real breakthrough "in mathematics" (something that, of course, we do not expect of him), there is also no chance of exceeding the limits of philosophy. With Badiou, philosophy remains well within the bounds of its traditional relations—French rather than Anglo-Saxon—and those of its history. Even the mathematics and logic that he introduces as conditions for philosophy, he considers under the authority of history, referring to them principally as historical formations. Whence his obsession with the "modern"—which, far from delivering itself from history, enchains and immobilizes itself within history. He dedicates himself once more to the reading of texts—in this case the mathematical text, but only insofar as it belongs to a ready-made history. After the reading of philosophical texts (Derrida), of Marxist texts on history (Althusser), of Freud (Lacan) and then of the Human Sciences (Foucault), the interpretation of great mathematical texts is invited to take up the baton. It is decidedly the case that here, philosophy (and in particular, French philosophy) falls back into its habitual, pusillanimous mistakes, refusing to experiment with philosophy itself in its being, rather than just its objects, languages and intra-philo-sophical becomings. This philosophical immobilization by way of history (as obligatory as ever, if often denied) is consummated, paradoxically, in a philosophy "without history" (Althusser and Badiou). A philosophy that ends up as a lazy queen, who hitches her carriage up to a pack of scientists, and can only get going by riding in the wake of the history of sciences. Accepting the need to reform itself, without making any attempt to reinvent itself, *it essentially re-acts to the sciences without acting, properly speaking, upon them—any more than it acts upon itself. What little action it has is limited to a reaction*, to varying its style and changing one or another of its forms, without abandoning its most traditional objectives, which are those of a superior authority, sometimes legislative, always imperial.

But onto this traditional manner, Badiou grafts another intention which is his own proper mark, neither a mere herme-neutic nor a true invention: *the re-education of philosophy—a*

concept that, for Badiou, has a globally political destiny.
Education and self-education take place through philosophy;
but re-education is a political action carried out upon philosophy
itself. And it is carried out in the form of a *pure mathematical
rectification [redressement], not to say a breaking-in [re-dressage].*
For here, the Cultural Revolution is no "circumstantial" topic for
intellectual debate, but a theoretical model that can be read transparently even in Badiou's most theoretical program. Up until
Badiou, philosophy was educative and pedagogical; with him,
it is re-educated by mathematics. And rather than an invention,
re-education is a particular type of *repetition*; one that seeks
to modify everything while conserving for it the destination
and the ends of philosophy. Here is the secret and the justifi-
cation of the initial (if exorbitant) cut between ontology and
philosophy—a cultural "matricide" with which Badiou-thought
begins. Is this not a new, Maoist, avatar of universal *Aufhebung*,
a manner of conserving philosophy through its re-education by
means of dismemberment, redistribution and subtraction? The
old duality surpassing/conserving is now relayed by conser-
vation/re-education. Philosophy will be forced out of itself, will
be forced to send its intellectuals to the narrowest and harshest
of schools. But this is still a way of conserving, in all essential
respects, its privileges.

This mathematical (and more secretly, political and "cultural")
program is of the greatest interest to what we call "non-philosophy." Non-philosophy, which seeks a way of depotentializing
philosophy and making another use of it, but via other, more
positive and less authoritarian procedures—formerly on the

"non-Euclidean" model, and at present through a scientific (physical) experimentation and performation of philosophy—not at all through a scholarly and "cultural" breaking-in. There are certain philosophers who dream of a new school, a new discipline, whether it be that of phenomenological description (Husserl), applied physical rationalism (Bachelard), the logical analysis of ordinary language (Analytic philosophy)... and now, that of the forced re-education of new intellectual cadres, who will govern through mathematics. These new cadres directing thought can only be philosophers—as we might have expected, ever since Plato. The re-education of philosophy conserves of the latter only its formal authority of doctrine and direction, its most authoritarian and most perennial aspect. It makes use of mathematics, and then logic, only as pedagogical disciplines safeguarding the correct image of thought—a project that some would not hesitate to call a bootcamp. We oppose to it a "non-" philosophy that conserves philosophy only qua "non-standard," in its effective methods and in the malleability of its materiality, entrusting new tasks—this time of invention—to the co-operation of physics and philosophy, rather than to the mathematical razor.

Whether it constitutes a new relation to philosophy or not, we must keep in mind this manner of treating the subject, in order to comprehend how non-philosophy—which, for its part, does not contemplate philosophy, but practices it otherwise, within a new, more experimental thought—can be interested in, but at the same time very much opposed to, a project like Badiou's. This project is bound to seem to it a half-solution, with all the drawbacks of every half-solution that hesitates to liquidate philosophical sufficiency, and is content merely to introduce a deviation into its classical objects—a kind of mathematical, rather than textual, deconstruction. Badiou ultimately re-normalizes that which, in his program, could have been "revolutionary," in the sense of Marx's oxymoronic "revolutionary science." He contents himself once more with a "revolutionary philosophy," a "cultural" revolution within the limits of philosophy, rather than a scientific and non-philosophical revolution *in* philosophy.

He achieves this at the price of what can only be called a pitiless purification and a philosophical voiding, neither of which are limited to his political declarations alone. Both as a result of the technical mathematical means and for political ends, he conflates the science of philosophy with the purification of philosophy. We shall discover the theoretical apparatus of this conflation in a total planification[1] that takes place as in a mirror, and through a certain torsion—specularity being the only means by which the void may act. An attempt to re-establish the supposedly original purity of philosophy, its correctness or its "line," after so many postmodern contortions, it is also a vast operation of the purification of philosophy, wherein the latter is reduced to its two major Platonic knowledges, convoked for a specular confrontation. We shall not be content here with alluding to Badiou's eulogy to emancipatory terror (or any number of other violent enunciations), so as to berate or make fun of them shallow-mindedly—with each philosopher accusing the other, banally, of terrorism. For he alone has had the courage to openly advocate it, to have assertively and consciously combined the conceptuality of Western philosophy with Maoism. The entire system, in its "metaphysical" depths, in its ultimate axioms, can be read as a manifesto of terror or of "cultural revolution" in philosophy. A terror with a twofold effect, consisting firstly in the putting-to-work of ontology, the major occupation of most "philosophers," which is now to be torn from the authority of philosophy and re-educated by mathematics; and subsequently in the return of philosophy as official Doctrine of Truth. Such a project can exercise a profound seduction over dogmatic minds, those exhausted by the apparent superficiality of the postmoderns, or those cynically celebratory of the excesses to which such a re-education might lead—we speak of this seduction "in full knowledge of the facts." But once this seduction has passed, are we obliged to return, head bowed, to the old humanist nostalgias, to liberal modernity—which, let us recognize, occasions a certain disgust not just for Badiou, but for every thinker who is not entirely corrupt? Badiou, also, has reacted to what is intolerable—but too fast and too harshly, with an appeal to the void, and with his own brand of nostalgia. From this misadventure we draw a cautionary principle that we call non-philosophy, but which does not exhaust the latter as science. Can one re-act without ceding too much to the nostalgia of the void? Is the void not the best argument for simply renouncing all action? It would be pleasingly paradoxical to make of Badiou's philosophy—so well-informed, so well-documented, so hardworking—a lazy philosophy. Of course, we shall not go that far. But it is worth emphasizing that in Badiou we find the old conjunction of three cults: that of personality (a philosopher of stellar rarity), that of the labor of the masses (as intellectual workers), and that of militant struggle (in the name of truth). That here the cult of personality becomes the cult of master-philosophers, the labor of the masses becomes that of intellectuals, and anti-capitalist militants confront "pétaino-parliamentarianism"—these transferences matter little. Yes, Maoism is a style that makes itself at home in the French context, donning the new clothes of "Badiolism." But we shall seek elsewhere, in the very principles of this doctrine, that which makes it so menacing. We must rethink non-acting [*non-agir*] in so far as, without re-acting to a conjuncture that demands nothing of us other than to re-act, and for this reason can lead to the void, only non-acting can act upon it.

A purification is always disquieting when we think of what it may have in store for humans. And Badiou's is so absolute that it is difficult not to feel threatened, despite his abstraction and his irreality. We must change arms, change strategy, oppose him with something other than those objections against "grand" systematic philosophy that were, in their time, Hamann's "metacritique of the purism of reason" (against Kant), Jacobi's apology for faith and the immediate (against Fichte), the individual and the instant in Kierkegaard, and real or generic man in Feuerbach and the young Marx (against Hegel). Nonetheless, these objections, each in their time, provided extraordinary armaments for the struggle against adversaries such as rationalism and the dialectic. There is no point in saying that we need a new "philosophy," unless we furnish it ourselves; but we must do so by taking the problem from another angle than that of such (often spontaneous and religious) protestations. We firstly need to defend ourselves against philosophical sufficiency by means of a new thought that would not be entirely of the philosophical genre, but without abandoning the philosophical arsenal altogether. A new critique that would not be just one more philosophical "critique" of philosophy, but an entirely other usage of the latter, opposed to its narcissistic auto-glorification and its dominant use of thought. With or without mathematics, in Badiou it is not a question simply of a philosophy *of* force but of a political practice of philosophy (Lenin) conjugated with the mathematical void, *a practice of the force of the void in all domains of thought, in the name of philosophy. Logics of Worlds*[2] tried to correct this impression, whose danger Badiou sensed—but the correction was carried out by way of exactly the same procedure: by purifying this time the intermediary stage of transcendental Logic, which he adjoins to the edifice whose completion (like a well-ordered table of contents), he believes, will suffice to attenuate the violence.

On the theoretical plane, we must resolve the fairly simple paradox that, in Badiou, the exceeding of classically "philosophical" means by science, art and politics extinguishes the philosophy it exalts; that the permanent defense of philosophy supposes that he purifies it, banalizes it and renders it decidedly meager. And on the more contentious plane of a generic ethics of philosophy, we must invent a defensive strategy that exerts the "force" of an ultimatum, but without violence. How is an ultimatum possible that is, in a certain sense, weak—a non-victorious force? *Non-standard Philosophy*,[3] which this essay accompanies, as the analysis of an at once limited and especially typical example of that which we refuse, proposes a more profound solution to this paradox. How can we oppose Badiou without entering into a mere "relation of forces," setting against him a force of the same nature as his own? All of these terms (purification, ultimatum, defense) obviously require further precision in order to avoid insoluble misunderstandings. To speak of a defensive ultimatum is strange if one thinks "relations of force" according to the French context (Nietzsche, Foucault, Derrida). But we have learnt to distinguish, on the model of physics (albeit in a very different way) between a "strong force" (that which Badiou intends to introduce into thought) and a "weak force" that we also call "generic"—that is to say, a force proper to humans rather than to Being. In reality, this generic force is not so much itself weak as it is a weakening of the strong force. There are ultimata, possibilities of defense or *last things* in other ways of thinking, and in particular (this is our solution) in a renewed "non-philosophy." More concretely: to protect philosophy against itself, must we purify it through the entirely specular mediation of mathematics, making of it a superior politico-cultural doxa that exalts mathematics as force of the void (like a kind of philosophical brainwashing)? Or should we rather aim for a scientific-*type* knowledge of philosophy, a knowledge that would no doubt be contingent, but which, this time, would truly escape such doxa? The spontaneous usage of philosophy involves an exaltation of force, of combat and of war that stems from certain of its origins, its axioms even, and which it appears to us impossible to reduce to a deviancy, whether this deviancy be a fascizing *objective appearance* as in Nietzsche, explicitly Nazifying as it has very precisely been shown to be in Heidegger, or Maoizing—all three of these consummated always in the condemnation of "democracy." The introduction of Maoism into philosophy cannot be a conjunctural accident, even if it is also a matter of a certain conjuncture; this would be to underestimate Badiou as a philosopher. No, it is an essential possibility of philosophy, one that philosophy makes available alongside others; a possibility first actualized by Plato, but one that is profoundly inscribed in the very axioms of philosophical decision, albeit more or less inert or apparently inactive at any given time. We require further details as to the new version of non-philosophy, and as to the analytic means that will allow us to detect in Badiou the indestructible residue of philosophy, and its conservation-reeducation by Cantor and Mao under the sign of Plato.

Introduction

What is it to "Badiolise"?
Prologue on the centre-stage

I thus propose to exhibit a tautology, to explore its hidden folds along with its manifest self-evidence: *Badiou is (still, more than ever) a philosopher!* Here, all the badiolisers of Paris and beyond burst out laughing: What a great discovery! Badiou, a philosopher? Isn't that what he never stops proclaiming and demanding of his readers—to recognize and contemplate (without making any particular effort other than that of reading) the validity of his doctrine? And it is true: for once, here is an authentic philosopher, all such predicates are welcome; but what renders the formula interesting or problematic is that he is a *philo-rigid* type in a discipline which, itself, is not particularly rigid. Maybe he will hesitate to read me since, after all, I demonstrate, with a certain doggedness that will be deemed futile, that he deserves more than full marks, that he wins the philosopher's grand prize (but does one award a grand prize to a Master?). He may even thank me (and send me on my way) for having attempted a work of synthetic elucidation of the principles of his work and of his philosophical personality. But all of these signs remain ambiguous. One of the principles of non-philosophy is that it does not at all suffice to call oneself a philosopher, in a more or less well-argued (but always sufficient) manner. This claim must be verified from without by *a science for philosophy* that will unmask not so much the vague and doxic claim of philosophy to be a science, as its narcissistic and specular pretention to be, precisely, a philosophy—and the right one. This will not, then, be a mediocre, critical and *sokalien* scrutiny—he is obviously beyond such things; but rather a quasi-psychoanalysis, making use of means other than the traditional hesitations and ambiguities of the concept of "philosophy" from which he fails to escape. If all my efforts only go to prove that Badiou is "still a philosopher," it is only insofar as he is not as much of a philosopher as he wishes to be... and that he is, more than he fears. It is thus not simply a matter of announcing what he himself never stops claiming, Philosophy-in-person, the Idea of the Master of thought surrounded by mediocre thinkers. An "Anti-Badiou" may seem to be an act of anti-philosophy, but that would be an overhasty conclusion—it would be to conclude from the paradigm to the essence. It must be agreed that, while non-philosophy has overtones of anti-philosophy, it cannot recognize itself in current anti-philosophy, whose origins are predominantly philosophical, and only secondarily scientific, or are scientific in too positivist a manner.

Take one of Heidegger's tautologies: the nothing nothings, speech speaks, the world worlds... *Badiou badiolizes?* A not entirely tautological formula, any more than the proposal that Hegel hegelianizes, or that Bergson bergsonizes. Its true radical extent is brought out by the following observation: *non-philosophy does not philosophize within philosophy, but only by using it,* and this is what allows it to treat apparently self-evident philosophical truths as symptoms. There are many ways of understanding and anatomizing this formula, *Badiou badiolizes*: according to journalistic accounts, media glorification, finally a great philosopher and militant has descended, in person, into the "political" arena. Precisely this point is a crucial question for non-philosophy and for its evaluation of the role of philosophers in their becoming-intellectual. But it seemed of more urgent and broader importance to write an Anti-Badiou than an Anti-Sarkozy—even if the first obviously implies the second. The "Badiou case" is certainly not a merely technical problem. It belongs to a betrayal specific to certain philosophers who, fascinated by the unexpected tandem Plato-Mao, and nourished on the largely justified hatred of liberal humanism, without further ado draw the conclusion that thought must be purified of every destination—I would say, at my own risk and peril (and being on guard against the right even more than the left), of every properly human "pre-" destination. Are we destined for history, for philosophy, for the world, have we been *sent*, probably from further afield than from our individuality, to wage a war in their name?

As one might expect, "Philosophy" [*la philosophie*] is a highly ambiguous expression, as often multiple as it is one. If Badiou is "still" a philosopher, and if this needs to be proved contrary to certain appearances, it is only insofar as we understand it in a sense that he does not wholly expect. And if he still belongs to this category, then we have at our disposal another concept wider than "philosophy" that allows us to exhibit the traditional and transcendent presuppositions that limit (perhaps necessarily) his usage of the concept of the pure multiple. As certain other philosophers have revealed with respect to language, being, the moral law, the a priori, etc., he intends to reveal that the pure or Cantorian multiple, not multiplicities, can and must be the condition, rather than the object, of "Philosophy." If only by virtue of this, his work is of great merit, and surely inscribes him into the history of philosophy insofar as the latter is made of singularities and interesting points. But his paradox consists in his being the greatest affirmer, advocate and celebrant of philosophy, while risking that he should end up without philosophy, without substantial thought—with nothing but a philosophy dismembered in its materiality and, what is more, purified in its Idea; consisting of nothing but proclamations, appeals to Ideas and to Masses, nothing but a few proper names (happy the rare, stellar elect that he recognizes, happy the rare truths that he certifies...). No philosopher has ever expended so much talent, energy and knowledge in celebrating the void purified of all things, except perhaps Socrates—does he not deserve an Aristophanes? And even then, Socrates began, pedagogically, by emptying things out to *make* the void; Badiou *ends* with the void, the void of Mathematics, of the Subject, of Truth, of Philosophy. Badiolism is an affirmation, a style, a posture, a statue that forms around it the type of circular void to which young badiolisers will gravitate.

Non-philosophy as democracy within theory

Thus, the situation is clear: on the one hand, a purification that is, in its own way, an "ethnic cleansing" (exclusively Greek) in philosophy; and on the other, what we shall call a "defensive ultimatum" against philosophical sufficiency's hold over humans. A new duality? Certainly, there is always a structure of paradoxical duality in any philosophical-type thought. But we suggest that *what is or would be self-contradiction within a philosophical position (which Badiou's position, like any other, is) can be reduced to the status of a simple duality, to a unilateral or non-dialectical paradox*—and it is this that what we call non-philosophy aims to achieve. This simple duality signifies that weakness, as excess of force over all force, far from opposing itself to the latter, head to head, subtracts a part of its force from it, depotentializes it. Non-philosophical utopia has never been about creating a new philosophy, and even less about unrestrainedly exalting "philosophy" through a flattening (whether intensive or topological) of its instances, of science, logic, subject, philosophy. Instead, it creates a new genre or generic practice, which might be called "philo-fiction." How to simultaneously amplify and weaken philosophy? It pursues these two apparently contrary aims through the invention of a device at once experimental and theoretical, physical and philosophical (at the same time modifying all of these terms). The old directive slogan of philosophy—to constitute itself into a "science of philosophy" which, without being positive, would make use of science and, without being transcendental, would make use of philosophy, so as to constitute itself from within and without itself—became possible and operative as soon as its model became quantum physics; and when, moreover, it found a type of combination called "unilateral," operating from within (philosophy) and without (the quantum model), that would not be philosophical but "generic." This combination is established experimentally in a matrix—an apparatus that treats dualities in a unilateral manner distinct from all philosophical dialectic. The solution lies in a new arrangement, unilateral and complementary rather than dialectical, of these dualities.

It is a matter of dis-closing philosophy without recourse to a theology such as Deconstruction, but instead by way of an ultimatum with a twofold function: to limit its claims, and to open it up as philo-fiction. Philo-fiction is something other than a new miscegenation of knowledges supposedly *at once* strangers to each other and given in themselves. It is a conjugation of disciplines outside their disciplinary incarceration as terms in themselves. These disciplines instead become parameters that will define a new space for thought. If there is an invention of new philosophical effects here, it is at the service of a usage other than that of a superior doxa; it is an unprecedented theoretical genre obtained by the quantum superposition of art, religion, technology, etc. with, each time, philosophy.

Non-philosophy has ceased to be a discourse of sense that could seem to be directly opposed head-to-head with philosophy; it has become what it always aimed to be—a generic science of philosophy. It was only able to do so by firstly availing itself of the means of a science capable of corresponding best to philosophy—a physics rather than a mathematics—and its kernel of quantum thought. But it still needed to find the type of organization that could legitimate the project of a quantum theory of philosophy. This came in the shape of what we call the "generic matrix"—a machine or experimental chamber wherein we bring philosophy and quantum logic, as simple variables, into a radical immanence that immediately operates as a critique of Badiou's "ontology of the void"—not through yet another criticism or deconstruction, but through a transformation of its apparatus and of the finalities that it upholds. Non-philosophy has become a machine that associates, in the form of variables, a philosophical invariant (reduced with regard to its sufficiency, of course), and a second invariant, that of quantum physics (also reduced with regard to its positive and encompassing mathematical apparatus). Here, we call that machine "generic," associating the philosophical-without-transcendental and the quantum-without-calculation, where the transcendental and calculation are no longer anything but means without proper ends. It can only be called "immanental." It has an aspect of materiality and an aspect of syntax, but intricated one with the other to form a machine of immanence. In a non-immanental machine like the computer, one juxtaposes the hard and the soft, matter and software, but not here. To mark that difference, we shall slightly modify the expressions of this duality, with the conceptual material or rather "materiel" [*material*][1] on one hand, and, on the other, not a software [*logiciel*] based in logic and mathematics, but a "quantware" [*quantiel*], so called since it is drawn from the form of reasoning proper to quantum theory. Under the name of quantware, we extract from positive quantum thought its rational kernel of non-positive thought, in the form of two fundamental principles of this physics: the principle of superposition and the principle of non-commutativity. Quantware participates in the materiel, and the materiel is organized according to quantware. This "economy" or functioning of materiel and quantware is one of what we previously spoke of as unilateral duality, something that makes sense only in terms of the functioning of the machine, not as a mere logical nor even philosophical syntax. Unilateral duality is not denumerable or formal. Thus, we can also say that the count-as-one does not apply to it, and the multiple of multiples even less so; it draws its resources from neither Cantor nor Cohen, but instead from the quantum model, underdetermined generically and no longer required to be a positive physics. The old non-philosophy is integrally conserved within this new machine, but is effectuated and completed, "fulfilled" in a certain way, by the borrowing from quantum physics of these, its fundamental principles. The *immanence of the One-in-One* that we previously spoke of prefigured the *superposition* that would give it its meaning and its possibility; and *unilaterality* announced *non-commutativity*—simply, we had not yet discovered that the solution to the coherence of non-philosophy and the means of its legitimation already existed, in another form, elsewhere.

We could say (no doubt simplifying hugely) that Badiou's ontology of the void is philosophy as context or vision of the world *for* mathematics, logic and finally information technology—but that non-philosophy is the context or the "vision of the world" *for* philosophy itself and the disciplines that are ordered by it. The former is a new philosophy of sciences, whereas the latter is a science of philosophy—but not through a simple inversion of the formula.

Philosophy as insufficient analysis of itself

The first thing that we question in all philosophy, and therefore in Badiou, is a self-analysis that is by definition insufficient, and which pays for this with a self-sufficiency. This is why, when philosophers look at non-philosophy, they see only a new philosophy that conceals itself or refuses to recognize itself as such. For they are happy to make a summary analysis of their own discipline, a spontaneous reading, without getting to the bottom of the mechanism of this thought. What justifies the existence of non-philosophy is first of all its new analysis of philosophy as a system of specular doublets—as a thought operating through double transcendence, even when it speaks of immanence. This is what is called the Principle of Sufficient Philosophy (PSP)—its self-encompassing character, among other things. Since philosophers see in philosophy only an indistinct mass contained within one unique encompassing whole, a milieu that is in itself homogeneous, and thus sufficient, within which they distinguish only secondarily regions, domains, objects, diverse frontiers, they lack a sensitivity for that permanent doubling (insensible or invisible since specular). They do sometimes grasp it, but only ever locally. If non-philosophy has made but one discovery, it would be that of the *universality* of this doublet structure. All the rest follows from this. We can continue to do philosophy, but it is an hallucination, a permanent doubling that does not know itself as such.

Phenomenology, indeed, did try to put thinking into direct contact with the thing or object—but not completely, since it kept the horizon of the world as ground. As did Wittgenstein, no doubt; and also Deleuze, although he simplified philosophical transcendence only to preserve it, after all, as specular torsion. The problem is that thought and the real must be "identified" by superposition, not by the Parmenidean Same that conserves their unity, identification or transcendence. As if the non-philosophical wave were kept enclosed and stationary by philosophical dams—the shores or banks of the river being, in reality, these dams in whose shelter one tries to survive. The Parmenidean Same is the mediatized mediate, the auto-mediation that substitutes itself for what we call the mediate-without-mediation that is generic man. In philosophy, contraries are reflected one in the other, rather than prosecuting, at least, a close combat (Heidegger). Even those who have seen the problem have grasped it locally, in this or that particular structure. Heidegger, Husserl, and all contemporary philosophers insofar as they have a certain relation to phenomenology, have done *phenomenology as a limited form of non-philosophy*. Philosophy has a twofold basis—it is a double cavern or double backworld. Deleuze makes the ground rise to the surface (simplification) only to molecularize it into a thousand surfaces; rather than the One-in-One, he privileges the metaphysical Multiple and the One of the old immanence as One-All. Whence the force of Badiou's argument against Deleuze qua philosopher of the One. But Badiou also remains in a prior philosophical position. *It is not that the One-all must be molecularized, but that the One-Multiple must be quantum-superposed*—something that results immediately in a change of terrain toward the undulatory. The ground, for philosophers, is a double ground, either directly so in classical philosophers, or indirectly so through the conservation of a positing either of the molecular multiple or of the materialist multiple. The ground conserves itself, and continues to constitute and to ensure the endurance of philosophical encompassing. In other words, with philosophers there is always at least a philosophical positing, either as Multiple or as One or as One-all, that conserves philosophical authority—and, in the end, we rediscover the Moebius band.

Doublets or doublings—it is all one, with minor nuances one way or the other. Philosophers have indeed initiated or re-doubled this doubling, molecularized it, torn or twisted it (Badiou). Derrida, for example, gave us the means to identify this problem: but in finally immediatizing the signifier and the absolute of alterity as affect, he still combines the Jew and the Greek, and makes the doublings quite manifest by multiplying them. But then why does he seek Levinas's most transcendent One, at the risk of thus tipping the balance in favor of the Greek influence? Is the half-Greek half-Jew ultimately a Jew?

Or ultimately a Greek as "same"? He is *différance*, of course. But since *différance* is the same or equilibrium, which still responds to the same ideal as Deleuze's reversibility, but simply in a distended or distanced form, it seems impossible to rid oneself of all trace of equilibrium as end, as implicit teleology. Only the Greeks and Levinas would be rigorous or coherent in their opposition.

To really place philosophy in question (even if we are obliged to make use of philosophical procedures), we must invalidate it in one blow and without remainder. We must presuppose every conceptual term to be already divested of all power. We must presuppose that the generic matrix is already given in the virtual state, and thus that philosophical objects are already reduced to the status of symptoms or mere occasions. This is only possible through a matrix that does not annul all philosophy. It should rather be the case that the encompassed that is philosophy is really simple, is a milieu deprived of its doublet—that it should be recognized at its very origin, from the outset, as a doubling of itself, and simplified.

This matrix must function in asymmetric but complementary manner, on immanence and transcendence at once. But on a superposed, not redoubled, immanence; and on a transcendence at first doubled, but then simplified or fallen into-immanence. This functioning, along with its effects, is, quantum-theoretically speaking, that of the undulatory and of its superposition on one hand, and that of the particulate freed from corpuscular double-transcendence on the other. The corpuscular is transcendence in the philosophical state, as doublet, with immanence playing a minor or secondary role, whereas the immanent undulatory is also a transcending, but a simple one (an ascending), super-posable and become under-determining. Why do we now speak of the Real as undulatory and particulate, that is to say as quantum, rather than as metaphysical? Qua simple terms or symbols, philosophy must become a quantum system of particulate superposition, functioning in the Real. The Real cannot be produced by a simple combination of symbols that run the risk of giving rise to doublets. Thus, the Real and the symbol—that is to say, thought—must be the "same" thing, but in a non-Parmenidean sense this time: precisely not identical, but *superposed*, in a milieu of interference and not of identification, a milieu rendered possible by the algebraic property of idempotence, of the fusion of terms. The Real *par excellence* is the undulatory-in-person as symbolic-and-lived [*vécu*] (the lived = the matter of the real), capable of including the ideal reality of the symbol qua noematic or immanent real at the same time as rejecting it qua in-itself or linguistic symbol.

This entire operation is what we call the under-determination of reality in itself, or "macroscopic" reality, by the Real. We shall also call it unilateral transfer. It consists in resuming [*relancer*][2] immanence through a new superposition, and at the same time in subtracting it from the macroscopic-type transcendence of reality that creates the illusion of reality in itself. Thus, it consists in subtracting a simplified transcending or all of immanence from double-transcendence and its doublets. The Real is and remains the immanence of a simple transcending, even in the reality that adds to it something

Introduction

different. This "different" is only different when the whole is seen from the side of this latter reality; the simple transcending of immanence does not itself see the fall or the front of the wave and thus the bilaterality of reality in itself (compatible with the Real since, from the outset, the Real or immanence commences as a transcending). There is no plane or plateau—only a semi-dualism or a unilateral duality, just a simple transcending or, again, an "ascending."

What is a defensive ultimatum?

There are at least two traditions of the "anti-." One is recent—religious anti-philosophy against the Enlightenment in the eighteenth century, or inversely anti-religion, which attacks a global thought or ideology; and then the contemporary anti-philosophy that emerges from the margins of psychoanalysis and which is a relatively structured thought. The other is named or individuated—a genre punctuated by *The Anti(ante)–Christ, Anti-Düring, Anti-Kautsky*. For, to be able to say "anti-," it is best to have a proper name as spokesperson of the ideology one opposes. Deleuze and Guattari's *Anti-Oedipus* is located at the midpoint between these two traditions. As is the present book, which attacks a philosophical personality recognized as very significant. It is thus indeed an Anti-Badiou, and critiques "a" philosophy through an individual in perfect concord with it. But Anti-Badiou prepares only a non-philosophy, and certainly not an anti-philosophy. The point that may attract most attention is not the main objective—which is, more broadly, a dismantling of the facilities, procedures and paradoxes of *every* philosophy, through the treatment of one particularly brilliant example. The rules of the "anti-" genre are not firmly established: there is the critique, the polemic even, but this is not a specifically philosophical genre—its rules are perhaps religious in essence, always a little *ad hominem*. And non-philosophy is precisely, if one might say so, *ad hominos*—it is an act of defense, not of intolerance; the defense of a certain human universality against an individual spokesperson of a tradition that is believed to place it in danger. This combining of the address and that to which it is addressed is the first aspect of an ultimatum of defense.

Qua critique of an individual, the "anti-" is a malicious genre with a certain caricatural aspect, and thus always a little unjust. It is important to mock the adversary, to make him ridiculous given the opportunity, and one thereby achieves various all-too-easy effects. If Badiou is really a "great philosopher," he bears overly apparent traces of it. The contrast between the academic master and the stellar celebrity, the mandarin and the emperor, produces a comical effect that Platonizing philosophers have never been keen on. Since everything is obviously stacked against us, the style as much as the basis of the thought, the writing as much as the relation to the real and to philosophy, the militant type, his posture of mastery, his intellectual becoming, his obsession with greatness (great art, great philosophy, great politics, etc.), it is difficult not to see oneself, faced with this Goliath, in the position of David—difficult not to imagine one of those antique philosopher clichés, crushingly dignified, impeccably trained, draped like those statues sculpted in eternity that Nietzsche evokes in relation to Heraclitus and Parmenides, and whose theatre Heidegger tried to rebuild for us. He wears all the signs of this greatness of manner—a little showy, in his "gaullian"-style proclamations, his grandiloquent and grandiose interventions, his masterful poise, his authoritarian style (and not only in his philosophy), his way of making a statue of his stature.

But the lampoon, as inevitable as it may be, is a poor weapon here, and very much secondary, since it will always be turned against whoever uses it. The adversary must be taken seriously, treated as exceptional. One does not write this type of work against any old inconsistent pop-philosopher, or against an essayist of very little philosophy one wasted an hour reading. The adversary must, in his person and in his consistent works, deserve one's addressing him with a certain type of "ultimatum." We should not believe, above all, that the character Badiou is the true object of the critique, nor even that we contest "his" philosophy—an absurd project when we know that a philosopher belongs only to himself and to *his* tradition. We blame the "philosopher" for nothing. Badiou, insofar as he strives to succeed Derrida and Deleuze, on the contrary, we blame him right down to his philosopher-sufficient essence—the essence, and not at all the way in which he puts it to work. He is the finest keeper of the flame and one of the most significant examples of what unbridled philosophy, and not just "unbridled Platonism" (Heidegger on Nietzsche), aims to be and can be; in his genre he is a paradigm, and a privileged object of study. Whence the other aspect of this text: an analysis of the ultimate basis of the "ontology of the void" (OV), and its confrontation with the non-philosophy (NP) that will serve us as a "microscope" with which to study it. This is the second aspect of this type of ultimatum: It must be argued, and cannot be established as a simple primary relation of force—above all when we are dealing with an author who is so "invested," and so consciously, in his work.

All the same, I do not intend to launch an interminable controversy, a dispute in the ether of the Idea and of the truth-in-itself, nor to "open up a dialogue." Because such a seasoned philosopher (and God knows, he is) will always rebuff any argument whatsoever. Philosophy is tailor-made for developing this pedagogy of the conceptual duel, even if it becomes a little more complicated with the postmoderns of the Judaic school. If he is a philosopher, he is sufficiently aware of the pointless nature of such dialogues, in which, however, he himself seems to delight more and more, in that fatal becoming-intellectual that sometimes lurks in wait for even the purest thought. The Anti- is not a dialogue. I oppose him to read in him—and this from the very outset—some axioms entirely different from his own and *whose type of weakness can no longer be measured against the force of his*—this paradox must be understood. But why cause such an affront to philosophers, with this refusal to dispute with them, equal to equal (or more exactly, unequal to unequal) if not to make of it a declaration of war? In the name of this non-philosophical thesis, that alone can justify such a refusal: *Philosophical dialogue is founded on an ignorance of the doublet structure of philosophy among philosophers themselves, who limit themselves to the objective appearance of their conceptual argumentation. This argumentation goes always to the "absolute," but never to the "radical" of thought. It contents itself with stirring up the sea of opinions, of which it makes a superior doxa.* Now, the sea of opinions is a sea before being a sea of opinions; philosophers stir up its surface without grasping the law of this agitation, reducing it at best to a marshy state—even, perhaps, the sharpest of analytics who do not fear the disorganization of their distinctions. If the philosophical dialogue is without any great pertinence for truth—each holding to his axioms and, above all, considering the element of philosophy as a "natural" milieu ultimately in harmony with all, a sort of superior *sensus communis*—then it is useful only for that which belongs to objective appearance: for explication, clarification and teaching, but that is all. And here is the third aspect of such an ultimatum: it is not a question of dialogue, of making theoretical compromises. Especially in conducting a defense case, we are not obliged to negotiate with those who make forcible use of every means at their disposal, and who know full well how to concentrate all of philosophy into a "Principle of Sufficient Philosophy."

But to know that all philosophy is discussable at worst, disputable at best (even the famous "absolute"), and endlessly invertible (apart from the stiff-necked opinion that can do nothing but oppose itself confrontationally to another) is an insufficient defense. We still need a principle of the defensive ultimatum that would "found" all of our axioms, or give them that type of weak force that hinders the strong force. This principle is simply that we have no other means of struggle at our disposal, the adversary having already used the whole arsenal, cornering us in retrenchments that, as far as we know, may be "our" last. With this *tabula rasa* of the ontology of the void, he helps us involuntarily to find "ourselves" and to support ourselves upon some other force that is no longer that of a weapon; a force that we *are* without knowing it, but which needed to be recognized. Perhaps he leaves us something like an "energy of despair" to fly or seek a problematic emergency exit, a sort of prior-to-first passivity. Since he makes of all the means—science, art, love, politics—an affair of force, placing them in the service of the militant Idea of philosophy, we also are condemned to consider that he has nothing but means; that the finest ends upon which history prides itself must re-enter into the rank of means. Means that it falls to us, then, to invent a new use for. This is not a nihilism, but what we shall call a generic (rather than philosophical) skepticism—the doubt permitted to humans as such, with regard to the highest ends that are proposed to them or imposed upon them. Since he manages to divest us of all our predicates and reduce us—word to the wise, take note—*to the state of a proletariat at the service of a mathematico-philosophical dictatorship that he places in a position to exploit human forces, we admit this divestiture by taking it at the face value of its possibility, and ask humans thus abandoned to recognize that they maintain the last line of real defense, what remains of the incompressible or inexploitable once philosophy is gone.* We call "Last Instance" this force that is non-commutable with the mathematico-philosophical complex. It negates of the latter only what can be negated—its all-encompassing double sufficiency (the Principles of Sufficient Philosophy and Mathematics). And it is this ultimatum or *last thing* that we put forward as generic science or non-philosophy, against the "Platonic" purification in which one would be wrong to see anything but one philosophical position among others, one more doctrine, even if everything in it is perfect and coherent, even if its author advances armed like the Hilbert of philosophy. We do not know whether, in Badiou, we see the future of philosophy already outlined; but we are sure, at least, that we see all of its past returning in a pitiless form—it is this that we must learn to identify in him.

There will be no cogito, no revolution, to allow us to pass from the absolute skepticism or nihilism of material force to the generic certainty that we-the-humans are the Last Instance against which even philosophies must measure themselves —at least no philosophical-type cogito, no transvaluation or revolution. The ultimatum thus has a last aspect, that of a wager: the wager of a simultaneous discovery and invention, upon the basis of a divestiture and of a wholly other use of these means. The philosopher wanted to monopolize them, but he offers them to us, without knowing it, qua disarmed. Badiou supplies a super-armament to philosophy—a re-armament, in truth, for militants; but his work, grasped otherwise, is also and at the same time a disarmament of philosophy. In it we find philosophy delivered entirely naked, divested of its finalities, clothed in only its narcissism and its materialist anti-humanism. Here is the last adversary, and here is the defensive weapon, the ultimatum that is humans taken as generic body. For a wager also, one must be a skeptic—but not necessarily a nihilist, as philosophers believe. The human genre cannot be nihilist—only the philosopher can.

Others will critique Badiou's works in the name of another philosophy sharing the same axioms (those of philosophical Decision), reinscribing them in a tradition, debating their political, mathematical and artistic statements. For our part, we make a parallel between them and "non-philosophy" as "generic science" or "non-standard philosophy." The latter is another practice of philosophy outside the norms recognized and accepted by those diverse traditions. We shall confront the most fundamental axioms of the two doctrines, with the twofold aim of demonstrating the profoundly conservative character of Badiou's thought, beneath its clothing (of such a "modern" cut), and of better understanding our own project. Unlike philosophical doctrines, non-philosophy conjugates the greatest admiration and the greatest resistance in its a priori defense of humans against true philosophical enterprises, such as that which it recognizes in Badiou's thought. After the era of the deconstructors (Derrida and all the others), that of the constructors (Deleuze)—and now, with Badiou, the era of the planifiers anticipated by Heidegger, and their master after Plato. Badiou is, of "current" philosophers, the sharpest intelligence, the fullest, the most ambitious and the most self-conscious. He has been able to make coincide, in his own way, philosophy's point of greatest exaltation and its point of maximum extenuation—a kind of auto-contradiction of its essence. Examining insistently philosophical Decision's excesses of sufficiency, in the past and to the present day, we never imagined we would find ourselves one day faced with a new Master of this decision, and what we consider his inhumanity—faced with a pure philosophical reaction on a grand scale, and aiming to save this thought with one last conceptual explosion, a greater than ever fire... work. His work might be read as a reaction, a long time coming, against the attempts to renew the philosophical gesture itself in its foundations, rather than merely reinforcing and buttressing it, as he continues to do for his part. And if this is not a dialogue, it is thus an ultimatum, but emitted this time from an acknowledged position of weakness, in an encounter with a position of acknowledged force. Despite all appearances, we are more comfortable conducting an a priori defense against the traditional assaults of philosophy than on the attack. An ultimatum signifies that we are not the mirror of the other. Very precisely, Badiou is a means for non-philosophy, not at all left to himself or to the force of transcendent finalities. Thus, this book is, above all, finally—and one must take it as such—a book in which non-philosophy explains itself to itself, but with the aid of a counter-model that it falls to us to transform. For, moreover, we need only consider Badiou in himself to see that he is a technically irreproachable philosopher, and an intelligence in excess of us in every way.

Organization of the book

This book is based upon a set of notes originally taken when *Being and Event*[3] was published, and on various other texts, reworked according to our own recent advances in non-philosophy. We have hardly taken account of *Logics of Worlds*, which extends Badiou's thought toward logic rather than a renewal of foundations. The chips were already down in a problematic that, in this second stage, aims only to extend its reading of, and its stranglehold on, different areas of knowledge. Despite its grandiose (if rather congested) deployment, it seemed to us less useful than the *Manifestos*[4] for our object, which was Badiou's philosophical prejudices, the bases of his materialism, and his conjunction of mathematics and philosophy. Working on the principles rather than on the surfaces, as a miner rather than a surveyor, we limited ourselves to what made up the substance of his problematic. Ultimately more interested in the problems than in the texts, we believe that it is a professor's business, not so much a philosopher's, to lose oneself in complete works—something that would prohibit one, moreover, from writing. To grasp the fundamental statements or ideals of a doctrine, it is even sometimes indicated to stop reading an author one admires too much—it is a question of freedom, of keeping a sharp eye, and of the possibility of working. What is more, many critical elements opposed to this type of philosophy were already present, but in a dispersed state, in *Non-Standard Philosophy*, the principal work that the present book accompanies, and which amplifies non-philosophy. These two essays were written more or less in parallel. In them we utilize a theoretical device that conjoins quantum-theoretical and philosophical principles both reduced to a strict minimum. To achieve a prior understanding of this technical device of non-philosophy, one is referred in particular to the introductions and the glossary of *Non-Standard Philosophy*.

The first chapter is preparatory, and presents some essential concepts. It is a brief thematic and descriptive parallel of the relation between the ontology of the void (OV) and non-philosophy (NP) for those unfamiliar with them. It reprises a text initially published under a pseudonym[5] and reworked here, and puts in place the most notable and central notions of these doctrines. It is a sort of compact *memento* that can be provisionally left aside.

Chapters 2 and 3, on the other hand, are polemical. They take up again the exposition of Badiou's philosophical personality, already evoked above, in relation to his decision understood as a "taking the side of the modern in philosophy," and his relation to science. His figure as a philosopher is significant, in concordance with his philosophical problematic, and merits one's interest in it.

Chapters 4 and 5 represent the "hard" theoretical kernel of this essay. They get down to the principles and the matrices from which OV and NP spring, and try to clarify the problem of subtraction. Chapter 6 describes the relation between philosophy and mathematics, each in the mirror of the other, and the effects of sterility and authority that emanate from this specularity.

Chapter 7 examines or recalls the quantum and ontological kernel of NP on the basis of the problem of materiality.

Finally, Chapter 8 draws out some consequences concerning "philo-fiction" as the only possible "documentation" of the Stranger, and concerning the generic ethics of philosophy.

1

A brief synoptic parallel

OV and NP seem opposed on every point

One takes as its basis the equation mathematical set-theory = ontology; the other takes as its scientific model the non-Euclidean theme, and later quantum physics. This opposition can be identified on four levels:

1   The governing scientific theme: on the one hand, a philosophy of the absolute Multiple and on the other, a non-philosophy of the radical One. It would be difficult, at least on an immediate reading, to imagine two ways of thinking more extreme, more opposed in the way they go about their common research into anti-contemporary radicality (philosophies of difference, Nietzsche, Heidegger, Wittgenstein, Deleuze, Derrida).

2 The object of thought: on the one hand Being, a set-theoretical and Cantorian recasting of the concept of "being" as primary, an other-than-fundamental ontology, a true ontological basis or condition *for* philosophy; and on the other, a relegation of Being to a secondary status, as instance of a wholly relative autonomy, in favour of the One as radical immanence or One-in-One, a radically non-objective instance of the Real; a decided, global refusal to understand the real as Being and consequently as the essence of thought, if not thought itself qua ontology (whether an ontology of "presence" or not).

3 The way of thinking itself: on the one hand, the militant advocacy of philosophy against the ideology of its "death" or its "end" (in which OV tries to include NP), with the caveat of an anti-Heideggerian dissociation of ontology and philosophy itself, a partition internal to philosophy (which reacts with the backlash of "meta-ontology") but whose origin is external (scientific); and on the other, a distinction that is external, yet immanent, between philosophy and non-philosophy; a distinction itself founded in an anti-philosophical or generic real. On the one hand, a philosopher-hero who inscribes himself in the Cartesian, Nietzschean and Mallarméan tradition of the heroic thinker; and on the other, a reduction of philosophical sufficiency (as double transcendence) to the status of a material or an object of a generic science of the "ordinary man" or the "human genre." Plato and Rousseau? Plato and Kant? Plato and Marx?

4 The conjuncture and the project: on the one hand, the question is how to succeed Heidegger by reprising the foundational Platonic gesture, how to avoid the Heideggerian extinction of ontology (in the form of the ontology of "presence," with all of its "postmodern" consequences); and on the other, how to elaborate an outside-philosophy thought, but one that relates itself to every possible philosophy, modern and postmodern, indifferently, as its material, rather than relating itself to a particular philosophical decision. On the one hand, in what way does the fidelity to ontology necessitate a new ontology, a Platonico-modern ontology; and on the other, how to deliver thought from ontico-ontological primacy, and more generally from all philosophical sufficiency, by elaborating a new thought adequate to a generic experience of the One-in-One—an experiment foreclosed to philosophy, but formulated using its symbols.

In any case, this antinomy, although real, must be nuanced and differentiated. Must we recall the trivial fact that, by definition, philosophers are not necessarily speaking about quite the same things when they use the same words? And that it cannot therefore be a question of fabricating a simplistic opposition that takes these two ways of thinking "to the letter" without a minimum of textual hermeneutics, as is always necessary when it is a matter of the historical emergence of doctrines? If there are oppositions, then they belong to the fundamental axioms of each doctrine; and even the very axioms themselves, if we are talking about language, are not of the same nature in the two cases: OV utilizes axioms that express the ontologico-formal decision of the Idea, whereas NP uses what it calls "oraxioms," which express the lived decisions of the generic subject operating the science of philosophy.

If OV and NP, at first sight, are opposed just as much as the Multiple and the One, it is precisely not a question of the Multiple and the One, in their interlacing and co-belonging, as in the metaphysics of presence or in Greek ontology before the more radical decisions of Plato, and as is once more the case after Plato and Descartes. OV frees the Multiple from all unity through the void and the empty set; multiple-of-multiples to infinity, Being contains only the multiple without unity. NP frees the One from the Multiple, from Unity and from their mélange; whence a One-in-One (we shall compare the formulae "multiple-of-multiples" and "One-in-One" later) or a real as immanence through and through or without-unity—an immanence radical-(to)-self rather than to the unity-form. The radicality of these positions at once hardens and softens their antinomy—an antinomy that cannot be thought according to the schemas (at least not the traditional ones) of philosophical antithetics. For example, both agree in assuming the "death of the Greek god of the One," even if they do not interpret this formula in the same way, the first reducing every possible One to the One of the metaphysics of presence and to its operatory content, the One of calculation, the second distinguishing from these bastardized or empirico-metaphysical forms a One-in-One that remains absolutely unthought by, or foreclosed to, all philosophy (including OV).

The four essential principles of non-philosophy

1   Immanence is radical and not absolute. It is produced by quantum superposition (the One-in-One) and not by philosophical identification, and is thus without philosophical division or decision. Unlike transcendence, it cannot sustain any amphiboly.

2   Radical immanence acts as uni-laterality or as Last Instance, non-commutable with any form of philosophical transcendence.

3   The analysis of the philosophical milieu as doublet or as diversely specular double-transcendence is fundamental. It is perceived in one way or another by philosophies as an appearance of simplicity, but can be perceived or becomes identifiable as doublet only under the principle of radical immanence or superposition. A complete analysis of the apparent simplicity and unicity of the philosophical milieu permits us not to reduce everything to the absolute, which is the myth that this appearance

of simplicity secretes; to refuse immanence as absolute, as do (in very different ways) Hegel and Spinoza, Husserl and Henry.

4 It is essential to eliminate the mélanges that are formed under a superior or transcendental unity. Every transcendental unity doubles itself in transcendence either as positive constituent (Deleuze) or as negative condition eliminated from the outset (Henry). The radical, for its part, does not eliminate the absolute, but allows for a genealogy of the absolute as immanental appearance.

Non-philosophy is the radical simplification of transcendence. Two authors have sensed this problem from different directions, and have approached this non-philosophical simplification: Deleuze via the plane of immanence without mélange, that is to say reduced to the specularity of a torsion; and Henry via a suppression of the unity of amphiboly and a return to a simple duality. These two positions present an oscillation between transcendental immanence as plane of torsion or body without organs, and immanence as transcendental ego.

Non-philosophy's solution is as follows: (1) To maintain the amphiboly of immanence/transcendence, but as a philosophical symptom to be analyzed; (2) To conceive radical immanence as materially itself a simple transcending; (3) But one that must be resumed and superposed with itself—and not as a concrete and autonomous instance, as in Henry; (4) To accord to immanence a quasi-subjective but generic function as non-egological Last

Instance, thus without making of it a superior and total unity, the body without organs, as divergence of a convergence, but instead as superposition. In their respective solutions, Deleuze and Henry still presuppose philosophy as constitutive, that is to say as transcendental triangulation. Deleuze makes of this a positive condition, Henry a negative condition. Non-philosophy avails itself of a scientific means to attack the doublets of philosophy or of its triangulation, via superposition and the quantum model. It thus possesses an external model, whereas Deleuze and Henry put philosophy to work upon itself—an auto-transformation or auto-interpretation.

Fundamental concepts

The objective of this first sketch of relations was to "scramble" first appearances, to complicate judgment. We can now take up these indications in more detail, to complete them.

1   The real is grasped either (OV) as Being, that is to say radical exteriority, not in relation to something else but in itself (qua multiple-of-multiples), or in a certain way as the immanence of pure transcendence, and thus freed from itself and absolutely autonomous; or (NP) as One-in-One, that is to say as radical immanence which is not immanence to an exteriority in itself, but immanence-(to)-self by way of interference or superposition of a quantum-undulatory type rather than

an in-itself type. The common adversary is transcendent unity—synthesis in general, difference in particular. But in the name of pure Being as multiple in itself, on the one hand, and of One-in-One as superposition on the other. In reality, the refusal of this common enemy bears to varying degrees upon metaphysical autoposition in the name of a certain identity (or non-difference) of the pure Multiple or, indeed, of immanence.

2   Either Being is primary, and enjoys a primacy over the rejected One, in the secondary and operatory strata of calculation or of the count necessary to the representation of the multiple; or the One is *prior-to-first*, but has no primacy or hierarchy over Being, which will from now on be "secondary," even if it is always primary and necessary for the distinct thought of representation. OV conserves the hierarchy but inverts it, "repressing" and displacing the One with the Multiple (but this inversion is also a real displacement). NP invalidates the hierarchy from the outset, in the name of the prior-to-priority or the subordinacy of order to the real, and thus distinguishes priority from prior-to-priority, metaphysical causality (first philosophy) from determination-in-the-last-instance.

3   OV and NP both refer to the composition of the Being of a certain multiple: either the Multiple-of-multiples as set-theoretical inhabitant of the void, or the microscopic Particulate as noematic correlate of the undulatory lived.

But whereas the Multiple and the void are primary, the Particulate is secondary and is posited in-One, or under condition of the One-in-One. OV proposes a concept of the Multiple of multiples that is numerical and then quantitative. Its empirical origin is the set, but the empty set, which "represses" or "prohibits" the set-form and thus conserves it, probably "truncated" or barred, in the immanence of the pure Multiple. NP manifests a Multiple that is not pure or absolute, but radical, or conditioned by algebra (the imaginary or complex number), without denying the set-form or the repressed unity (whose absence or presence is not the problem here). The essence of this Multiple lies in the immanence of superposition, its simple transcending such that it falls into-immanence. It no longer has a transcendental identity, much less the transcendent identity of the repressed set-form.

4   Under the name of "ontology," OV defines a new form of materialism, by substituting for the old "empiricist" vocabulary of metaphysical materialism the post-Heideggerian transcendental vocabulary—in particular the terms of Being, the One and the Multiple— and sometimes the Sartrian terminology of the "in itself." This is a "materialism" insofar as it is a question of the identity "in itself" of pure transcendence, or the Multiple "in itself," of Being outside all "ontological difference." NP defines a thought that, as immanental and not using only

transcendentals, refuses all philosophical (idealist and/or materialist) decision, and roots itself in the sole real-One, while remaining in a relation that is unilateral or without relation to... philosophy in general, to any philosophical decision whatsoever or to the world.

The first turns Platonic idealism into a materialist position; the second dissolves transcendental realism into a lived materiality, a duality of the real-One and of the unilateral thought that flows from the One.

The non-epistemological relation to science

OV and NP do not think philosophy without also thinking its relation in principle to science—even if they posit different relations between themselves and science. Epistemology in all its different forms, all differential to varying degrees (idealist, positivist, rationalist-applied, critical, etc.), is deprogrammed and eliminated as a sterile or fetishizing combination of philosophy and science. They oppose to it a certain "fusion" of science and philosophy, rather than a difference: either (OV) an identity with science which (by way of a meta-ontology) separates ontology from the rest of philosophy; or (NP) a radical fusion (in a Last Instance) of science and philosophy—a fusion "under-determined" by science, and which guarantees the undivided immanence of philosophy and permits a generic genealogy of the latter.

The suspension of the "epistemological" combining of philosophy and science supposes new relations between the two: OV detaches ontology from philosophy proper. But it treats ontology as a secondment of philosophy to science, or better, as an identity of philosophy and science. It is a matter, as far as science is concerned, of a particular but supposedly paradigmatic science (mathematics—and, within mathematics, axiomatized set theory); and as far as philosophy is concerned, of a new distinction imported into it through its identification with science: the distinction between philosophy and meta-ontology—as if science, dividing up the philosophical tradition into ontology and philosophy proper, had to redivide the latter into "meta-ontology" and philosophy. These refoldings represent a residue of the doublet and of autoposition, not yet radically eliminated. NP takes philosophy globally as ontology and with ontology, without separating them, and treats them in relation to a scientific thought grasped in its essential operations (the axiomatization of hypotheses, induction and deduction). But it has passed through two distinct positions as to their relations. *Philosophy II*[1] supposes an affinity of the vision-in-One and scientific thought rather than philosophy, and thus attributes a certain primacy (later called "prior-to-priority") to science over philosophy. Later works (*Philosophy III*, including *Théorie des Étrangers*)[2] give further nuance to this preferential bond, which was still close to OV's solution. The vision-in-One is as indifferent to science as it is to philosophy, but it always determines a non-philosophy that is equally a non-science (thus we refuse Deleuze's objection). Non-philosophy, a thinking adequate to the real-One, takes as object-material the different philosophical relations between science and philosophy (of which epistemology is one), and elaborates on their basis a "unified Theory" (unified, but not unitary = philosophical) of thought as identically philosophy and science, removing their autopositional character, or its residual form present in OV.

To the four "truth procedures" (of which science is one) that sustain philosophy proper (OV), NP opposes an open multiplicity of "unified theories," each of which takes as object-material the relations between the fundamental and the regional (philosophy + a determinate region of experience: philosophy and politics, philosophy and psychoanalysis, philosophy and ethics, philosophy and art, philosophy and technology, etc.). Science has no exclusive privilege in non-philosophy, except for that which flows from its privileging within the philosophical material (which, precisely, is no more than a material). Positivism and scientism, which are both philosophical possibilities, are suspended as far as possible. Finally, where OV makes use, in traditional philosophical manner, of a determinate scientific theory (Cantor, Cohen), NP instead requisitions scientific *styles* (non-Euclidean axiomatics and various other models: fractal, Gödelian, etc.). In its most recent stage (*Philosophy V*), it also mobilizes a determinate science, quantum physics.

The relation to Marxism

OV refashions set theory into a quasi-dialectics, Platonic rather than Hegelian—a dialectics for a quasi-matter or "in itself" of the Multiple, a dialectics that recuses empiricist and sensiblist materialism. It refuses in general the difference between materialism and the dialectic, positing instead their identity, which supposes the identity of the Multiple and the Void—a mathematical materialism transcendent to the "subject" it determines. Such is the materialist Dialectic. NP, on the contrary, reactivates and transforms the themes of historical Materialism: (1) The real as immanence, immanence as radical or unilateral "indivi-duality"; (2) Thought defetishized as the force-(of)-thought [*force (de) pensée*] (cf. "labor-power" [*force de travail*])[3] that (3) effectuates the real-One as determination-in-the-last-instance; (4) A "science" ("unified theory") of the superstructure (philosophy, in its complete concept, not qua "ideology"). Both OV and NP convoke and partially take upon themselves a Marxist heritage that they do not wish to leave dormant, but in doing so, refuse all "neo-Marxism."

Both therefore maintain a relation to Marxism that is privileged but dosed to different degrees with the latter's death and survival. OV announces the death of Marxism, and privileges instead the materialist Dialectic and a Maoism transformed both on their materialist side (Being or the multiple in itself) and on their dialectical side (set-theoretical multiplicity). NP instead maintains a relation with historical Materialism, transformed on its materialist side (the real as materiel), on its historical side (philosophy as encompassing horizon or universal of human practices), and finally in its syntax, which is no longer dialectical-ideal via over-determination, but unilateral duality via under-determination.

The relation to philosophy

OV claims philosophical sufficiency, but on condition of relieving philosophy of ontology, which is now operated via mathematics. On one hand, philosophy is reduced, in its relation to mathematics, to a meta-ontology; on the other, it is reduced, in its relation to the four "truth procedures," to a simple "inventory" function—that is, to the function of a widened synthesis or weakened (weakly encyclopedic) system, whereby the antique function of the One excluded from ontology returns. Thus, there is here a basis for philosophy that is "non-philosophical," in the sense that it is "merely mathematical." It is also a "non-philosophical" basis of philosophy in the sense that the latter can identify itself in it, in the form of its meta-ontological relation. So that the non-philosophical is not thematized as such, but operated as a subtractive, or even "negative," critique of presence. NP speaks of all of philosophy, without parts, but speaks of it as mere material, without validity over the real-One but validated as object of a non-philosophical usage. OV still maintains a philosophical relation to philosophy via the subtraction of science, whereas NP maintains from the outset a non-philosophical but positive relation to philosophy. In one case, "non-philosophy," determined as mathematical ontology, is still governed by philosophy qua meta-ontology, but in a relation of identity rather than of difference. In the other, the non-philosophical use of philosophy amounts to universalizing thought beyond philosophy, and correlatively to finally generalizing the latter, generalizing any philosophical decision whatsoever, to all of experience, as an a priori. Either philosophy must be supposed to be globally pertinent, as per its traditional claims, or else we must consider this a matter of a mere claim that must be limited (as to the real) and legitimated (by restricting it to experience). Either there is something "not philosophical" (rather than a non-philosophy) that remains partial, external (and) internal (without difference) to philosophy and divides the latter—this is OV's solution and, in another way, Deleuze's solution as to "non-philosophy"; or else non-philosophy is global (in the exact sense that, via its identity, it is valid for and applies to every philosophy and all of philosophy), external and heteronomous (and) immanent—thus preserving, or rather necessitating, the identity of philosophy.

The relation to philosophy no longer has the simplicity that certain slogans or appearances might suggest. OV does not maintain entirely or without distinction a homogeneous relation of affirmation to philosophy that NP would call "sufficiency," of the "all-philosophy" type (despite its "manifestos for philosophy"). In OV, this relation of philosophy to itself is internally divided or split by science (mathematics), as philosophy identifies itself with science by depriving itself in some way of its traditional ontological heart, whose function is now assumed by mathematics. Ontology then becomes a special form of "non-philosophy" in the very interior of philosophy. NP does not maintain, as certain appearances might suggest, a relation of negation to philosophy, but a positive relation of generic usage, and one of suspension in regard to its pretended sufficiency for the real. In OV, the distinction passes by way of two "parts" of

philosophy, which globally conserve its authority along with a
prohibitive or truncated form of its sufficiency. In NP it passes
by way of the "all-philosophy"—that is to say the "Principle
of Sufficient Philosophy" and the identity of philosophy as
mere material or occasion. One opens from the interior of
philosophy onto the exteriority of mathematics; the other opens
up philosophy from outside to a thought that is nonetheless
immanent (only the radical immanence of the One-in-One can
be heteronomous to philosophy and nevertheless "act" on it).
OV affirms philosophy while sacrificing ontology to science,
whereas NP neither affirms nor denies philosophy, but sacri-
fices its global sufficiency to a quantum-type "superposition," a
superposition via the radical, albeit heteronomous, immanence
of science and philosophy.

Both doctrines pose the problem: how to conserve philosophy,
what sense to give it after the "death" and the "end" of philosophy?
OV responds by reaffirming the ontological claim that was
philosophy's, but making philosophy assume it, this time,
through mathematics, and by confining the traditional activities
of philosophy to the constrained function of the "inventory"
and "arrangement" of truths produced elsewhere. NP responds
by globally diminishing, across the whole extent of philosophy,
the latter's claims, but by limiting them to the sole experience
of constituted knowledges, assures them a certain legitimacy,
like a transcendental ("immanental") deduction of philosophy
(of the identity of philosophy). OV refuses philosophy this
identity and amputates it from its essential part. So that in
reality, it is above all OV that poses the problem of conserving

philosophy, responding by amputating its sickly member (the philosophical ontology of "presence") and issuing it with a mathematical prosthesis; whereas NP seeks to assure it of its integral life by suspending that which bars its "real" claim or stance, renouncing this process of self-amputation that already constituted the whole traditional life of philosophy in any case. OV begins by cutting into philosophy, between two of its parts or functions, and claims thereby to have saved it, whereas NP refuses to decide (to philosophize), and on the contrary necessitates its identity—only distinguishing, in view of the latter, between philosophy and its tendency to claim over the real. One is a hero who comes to the rescue of an imperiled philosophy that he himself continually menaces; the other a redeemer who, since he thinks it a priori "saved," sometimes appears to forsake or refuse it. Philosophy was already saved, but we did not know it because we were *in* philosophy, and philosophy hid its true face from us...

2

Taking the side of the "Modern" in philosophy

The "Modern"

The birth of a new and great philosophy that would be in the spirit of modernity—that is to say, a purge "for our times" and its errors—was bound to appear unexpected to an epoch that would see itself as postmodern. *Being and Event* offers the whole panoply of the reasoning of the "Moderns": a certain description of the unsatisfactory conjuncture and a departure from it; the observation that "our times" are lacking in true philosophy, along with the vague and ideal thesis that a philosophy is a philosophy "for this time"; the twofold appeal to that which founds modernity: mathematics in the form of the Cantorian creation, and the theory of the subject in the form of the

Lacanian creation; the exaggerated spirit of axiomatic decision and the equation to think = to decide, in relation to the pathos of the conjuncture; and finally, all the values or means of the contemporary, but re-inserted into the "modern" discourse (the signifier and the symbolic, the impossible real, foreclosure, structure, the multiple, the event, etc.). And then, adding to the clarity and neatness of these positions, the systematic and coherent development of theses, the breadth of vision, and (to repeat what so many others have said) the courage of thought. This book "arrives" in timely fashion, and is in many respects a miraculous book, just like any great work. And like all "true" works of philosophy, it begins its "fall" or completion [*chute*] well; it seeks to negotiate it and to create its own conjuncture.

Those who had imagined a linear development of thought, a definitive solving of problems or an obsolescence of philosophy, were surprised by certain regressive and, all in all, conservative aspects—not at all "modern" in a more common, that is to say more contemporary, sense. Badiou sets himself to proving, brilliantly, that Heidegger's poetico-Aristotelian reactivation of philosophy can be succeeded by a mathematico-Platonic reactivation, and of proclaiming at the same time a definitive ruling on ontology. Such is the contradictory law of every philosophical "return," and of this one in particular; of that Platonic and Cartesian sentiment of re-inaugurating philosophy once, finally, and for all time—a procedure that another modern, Husserl, made his own. In reality, Badiou maintains a complicated relation to philosophy. On the one hand he is not "interested" in it in any intimate manner; he is interested in literature, politics, mathematics and love. But he saw in philosophy a way of bringing together and planifying this disparate set of activities and talents. And maybe he is justified in this—philosophy has always been more or less a catchall, a corral for scientific statements, for virtuous and political slogans found along the road of tradition, all the while being also that "bone-bag" (Plato) that collects up the cadavers of humans. But if Philosophy is nothing but this, then why ceaselessly overburden us with it, why make a slogan of it? Especially as what really motivates him are the three or four "truth procedures." About philosophy he has, fundamentally, nothing very precise to say, no more than he has to say about the Emperor. He has something to say about its logic, its truth and its subjectivation—and always to celebrate the Truth, the Idea and the Void. His principle is to avoid speaking of philosophy itself until it is no longer possible to do otherwise—but with what vigour he does so then... He practices it *in extremis*; it is a bunker or a wall that he guards like a flag. On the other hand, his combat for philosophy is strategic: it is a matter of struggling against his times and what they herald. There is something chivalrous in this combat—he defends a distant, evanescent philosophy with a sort of courtly love; he has placed his faith in it, seeing off with the back of his hand everything that claims to approach it from afar or even from nearby, through default or through excess, through lack or repletion. As soon as the conjuncture seems to present the opportunity, he writes a new manifesto to defend the outraged dignity of philosophy. His need to "explain" himself to the most paltry of media intellectuals becomes a little disquieting and confirms the old ideal of the philosopher, no longer counselor of the Prince at best or global intellectual counselor to the State at worst, but (is this so different, however modern it may be?) master of militancy and of taking sides. Even his "reconciliations," with Deleuze and Derrida, for example, are dubious, since they are often posthumous. I put this amiability down to the benefit of wisdom, or of age, now that he has succeeded them on the stele of philosophy. Having seen how he treats Deleuze, countermanding the complexity, simplifying the duplicity of his position, I ask myself what fate he has reserved for his contemporaries in his "portable pantheon." In fact, here is a triply mischievous formula: the "pan" or the all, the "theos" or embalming death, and the "portability" of the worst kinds of doxa—things he quite rightly detests.

Modern, but not contemporary

To be declared or recognized as a "great philosopher," one necessary condition, among others, is to be a counter-current against the contemporary. Although he wishes himself a bloc of eternity, the risk for Badiou then becomes that of still measuring himself against the immobile ground of the current itself, or of resisting traditional criteria too weakly. This would make precisely for a "modern philosopher," in many senses of the word. Contemporary he is not, except insofar as he introduces new means clothed in an old skin. For it is always means that make for contemporaneity, just as ends make for modernity or antiquity—for tradition, in any case. So long as one finds the fruitful generic finality proper to these means, rather than the traditional one that he imposes upon them as texts to read or decipher one more time. What purpose do Cantor and Cohen serve, then? To modify the cartography of philosophical thought, to be the object of a new "hermeneutic"-*type* activity, to conserve the old philosophical finality but merely in a limited form; not at all to actively transform philosophy and its own finalities. There are so many impressive means to explore (or to make one read) that he does not think of changing the classical destination—that of a text to read, that of philosophical sense. This outer shell he conserves like a wineskin, and he drinks this philosophical cup to the dregs of the Idea. An authoritarian militant, nostalgic "for our times" but not at all our contemporary, he comes decidedly from afar, he is in spirit entirely outside our times.

I do not define the contemporary by way of any finality whatsoever, any teleology found and repeated, even a "modern" one. Badiou is "finalized-modern"; he revives the prescriptions of a certain teleology, which we shall reveal to be circular and transcendent. The modern is an affair of philosophical finality and thus of return. The contemporary is almost without finality—it is an affair of means, of means offered by the conjuncture—a question of usage and of comportment. It is defined by an intra-temporal order that supposes the arrow of worldly time oriented from the future toward the past across the present. The productive future, or rather that which non-philosophy calls *futurality*, without being a mere orientation

or an "occidentation," would be a certain break in the circle—
more complex than modern "priority," because it would be that
of a prior-to-priority or of the Last Instance. The future is only
(if one might use such a bizarre expression—it will be justified
by the imaginary number used by quantum theory in the wave
function) the *quarter* (of the circle) of eternity and of finality; at
best half of it, but certainly not its totality, with the inversions
of sense that such a totality would contain. It concerns only
the usage of means in view of the invention of existence. As
the category of the contemporary and of its futurality, the Last
Instance is that dimension that does not bring to presence or one
of its deconstructed modes, but puts into unilateral complementarity, knowledges deprived of all external or internal finality
and transformed into mere means—means that must contribute
to creating a new generic end with which, this time, they are not
commutable. The two greatest thinkers *of* the contemporary are
not moderns, but Marx and Freud, who knew how to conjugate
contraries, and not dialectically—so it is natural that they have
become unbearable for most of "our contemporaries."

Thus, knowing nothing of the category of the "contemporary," which is opposed directly to the tradition and to
its multiplicity, including the modern, Badiou is one of the
most conservative and regressive philosophers that could be,
dressed in the deceptive habits of modernity. We all know that
Modernity, even in the guise of "Platonism," is a tradition, just
like Aristoteleanism or Phenomenology. Whereas the contemporary is the generic primacy of means over every primary
finality, and consequently their indirect combination (between

means). Ultimately it is a de-localization and de-temporali-
zation of their effects of residual finality and subjectivity (an
enterprise that we name, for our part, "quantum," in the new
context of NP). What point is there in affirming the multiple, if
one does so only to extend its materialist destination to the void,
or to limit the use of philosophy to the void of truth—in either
case, to a dessicating abstraction? The multiple is a multiple
of means. Once more, we must find a thinking of the multiple
that does not make it back into an empirico-transcendental or
mathematico-materialist thesis. A change is called for *in the
usage* of traditional mathematical and geometrical means that
are too attached to an authoritarian and harassing philosophy, in
favor of the suppleness and the plasticity of a lighter apparatus—
for example an algebra, as used in quantum thinking.

Badiou wishes to start over, and thus to turn back. But not
too far—not to the very basis of the tradition like Heidegger;
he refuses the pre-Platonic style of Deleuze's physiologism or
organicism. But why seek to return only to Plato, and only to
set out once more in a direction neither entirely parallel nor
wholly opposed to his? Because Plato named "philosophy"? Or
rather because he is the first genius of planification? Because for
Badiou, the means, or the use to which they are put, is universal
planification. Plato is already a latecomer, like every modern.
Precisely a modern from after myth, and a mathematician from
after physics, he possesses the art of ordering and hierarchizing
the riches of the past—in a less scholarly way than Aristotle,
that is the only difference. Planification is the Moderns' form
of memory, a profligate deployment of spaces and plans so as

to save, conserve, or raise up the past. Which is only one more finality and the vehicle of all finalities, rather than something that could draw out new inventions from them. If philosophy as double transcendence is imaginary in the specular sense, then non-philosophy opposes to it the algebraic imaginary and its quantum superposition. This is what the vision-in-One would say, and has always sought to say; vision-in-One as a method that struggles systematically against doublets, that separates philosophy from its double (the world) and simplifies it. This is the vision-in-One of philosophy.

The defense of philosophy as desire for memory

In a sense, there is no interest in defending philosophy out of duty, or even out of a desire for memory, if one produces nothing more than new readings of the tradition, judging or deciding what is good or bad according to highly ideal criteria; if one understands nothing of what it is (Deleuze and Derrida were more attentive in this respect); if, rereading the past on the basis of a "new" decision, one limits oneself to housekeeping, and to instituting oneself as a Platonic tribunal. In that case, the interest lies only in a purification that looks toward the past. Badiou continually risks being confused with the *worst* defenders of philosophy, or even, more subtly, with its perse-cutors. Certain of his readers ask whether this prodigious all-out deployment of means only goes to arm one more Don Quixote.

In all domains, except for literature and politics, but certainly in mathematics, the generic procedures, and philosophy, he is a militant of theory, who has perhaps stifled the proper concreteness of philosophy by dint of cultivating innumerable theoretical means that he employs precipitately, to take the place of concrete philosophies. As to positing the principle that the philosophical domain must retreat, ceding its place to the generic, we are entirely in agreement. But why such a violent purification, in which the generic functions as a weapon of mass destruction? Perhaps it is not possible to avoid going all the way to the extenuated end of the Idea, but in that case why oppress us with this philosophy that he wears like a bandolier? One would almost think he was apologizing, or at least protecting himself *in extremis* against himself.

He calls for the defense of philosophy *in every possible case*. A necessity that is contestable with regard to the materiality of what he has to defend, and with regard to the finality of the simple means that it also is. Is the emancipation of the philosopher worth anything if it is not directed, at least "in the last instance," toward that of humans (who are not limited, need it be said, to self-declared militants)? It falls still to a (non-) philosophy to "disentangle" all of this so as not to reconstitute a worn-out finality. Too often, in NP, these two defenses have been understood as operating in opposite directions, in a misinterpretation of the polemic that NP carries out against philosophical sufficiency. But it is a question both of freeing philosophy from its self-reference and from its magical confinement in its own circle. Its liberation from itself is the occasional condition for the liberation of humans, but the liberation of humans is the under-determining condition of that of philosophy. The interpretation of these relations as the circle of a unique divided condition, set against itself by means of some torsion, is a transcendental-type appearance. What seems to be a circle is in reality broken, opened up (rather than distended) between a cause in-the-last-instance and an occasional cause (between a prior-to-first cause and a first cause). More than distended, as a topological and plastic body would be; instead, open as a "unilateral duality" whose identity is inalienable in duality, or whose prior-to-first term is immanence through and through, and transits every transcendence with radical immanence. This distribution is not just another case of the transcendental; we shall call it "immanental." It is a transcendence fallen into-immanence, where immanence is not reciprocally alienated in the unilaterality that it determines.

Whence we can identify between us a series of differences that are not at all symmetrical: to the planification that, in Badiou, replaces the old dialectic, I "oppose" unilateral duality; to the exception of the Idea that is the complementary idealist part of materialism, the prior-to-first exception of the human in the world; to the materialist position, lived materiality; to the "circumstance" the conjuncture; to corpuscular Being, the undulatory One-in-One; to the Cantorian multiple, the particulate multiple; to the stellar brilliance of philosophy, a quantum of the flash of the Logos; to mathematical formalism, a generic and materiel formalism with no residual bond to real arithmetic; to the mathematical Idea that one would contemplate to save oneself, the humans who alone will save themselves; to topological torsion, the "quarter turn" and the vector; to Plato (a gnostic who betrayed the gnosis of which he was capable, in favor of Pythagoras and transcendent philosophy, as Badiou does in favor of Cantor), I oppose the figure of the philosopher as demi-god, inexperienced and precipitate. It remains to discover who to oppose to the world, to the rather botched work of a God who is mischievous and (himself also) inexperienced.

A master of planification

If NP is an ongoing process, in the form of a series of oceanic swells, OV is, if not a system, at least a long-planned and organized state of thought. Badiou is a great planifier—this is his way of legislating. His ambition begins with literature, with, in the background, the school of mathematics. One of those he admires, Sartre, turned toward the human sciences and psychology, whereas he engages in the hardest and the most technical sciences, drawing secondary benefits from them (a certain distance, a seriousness, an authority, an elitist obsession with rarity) which he does not hesitate to demonstrate. On this basis, he deploys the spectrum of talents that make for the type of master-thinker that French intellectuals fantasize about. And this time it is indeed a matter of an authentic master and thinker—and, at last, a French one. Just as he managed his interests and talents as a writer, a dramatist, a militant, a mathematician and finally a judge dispensing honors or "truths," with a certain paternalism, in the form of various proper names, so he has been able to draw out the best part of academic, media and above all publishing institutions, placing himself at certain of their central points, at the crossroads that would assure him security and sovereignty. In a sense, Badiou's entire thought seems tailor-made to dress the statue and validate the stature of sufficient philosophy, not to dedicate itself to any object (such is the poverty of his conception of philosophy). His purism of Ideas, of the subject and of stellar events, his judgments of rarity seemingly difficult to square with a communist doxa to which he prefers the communist Idea... Erecting a lofty image (somewhat narcissistic and specular) of himself, does he not dream of being to Plato what Lacan was to Freud? His theoretical planification is just as impressive. But in any case, we would not have evoked his personality in this somewhat acerbic manner did it not find its perfect continuation, with the greatest coherence, in his theoretical oeuvre, which is a mirror for it. It is this oeuvre alone that really interests us, and despite ourselves, we cannot begrudge him our admiration for it. But this only makes all the more total the contrast of contexts with NP, all the more crushing the comparison with the solitude of the latter, its hesitations, the institutional and editorial censure it has suffered since its birth and still suffers today. In contrast to Badiou, NP is but a sum of margins (religious, economic, social, geographic, institutional). Even if it succeeds in changing the object of experience according to the theoretical conjuncture, its style is less that of the planification of strata of knowledge and power, between the figures of Hegel and Deleuze's thousand plateaus,

than the radicalization of the desperate situation of man in the
world—a globally "religious" inspiration, if you insist, between
mysticism, gnosis and Christianity. How could we not put
ourselves on the line, against Greek purification and "great
philosophy," through recourse (once more, it will be said) to a
certain Christianity? In any case, as we elaborate in *The Future
Christ: A Lesson in Heresy*,[1] ours will not be the Christianity of
that other great purifier, Saint Paul.

By virtue of this abstraction and planification, which
condition one another, philosophy believes itself able to resolve
certain ethical difficulties. On the one hand, the abstraction
of too narrow a conception of the generic that makes it hold
in too high an esteem the solitude of a "set" of individuals,
Strangers; or again, the Idea of the Immigrant, parallel to the
Idea of Communism, rather than that of humans as they exist
in-generic-body or -stance. The question of what is concretely
generic is one of the fundamental points of the OV/NP
conflict: is it the old philosophical individual in the *position* of
transcendent subject as "humanity function," or instead indivi-
duality as existence in-generic-body or *-stance*? On the other
hand, OV's planification renders sublime the most problematic
philosophical acts if they took place in the sphere of doxa, and
permits philosophy to save itself from more "base" attacks.
Nor does Badiou escape the benefits that planification and its
"absolute" radicality procure—the benefits of a good conscience.
But why would a Greek purification in philosophy be more
acceptable than such a purification in the sphere of the City or
in history? We do not believe in this way of sheltering its dignity,

distinguishing so easily between planes of heterogeneous ethical behavior, where what is deplorable in one is not, is less so, or is even necessary, in another. Religions, Platonism in part, and even Marxism, with its partitioning of "instances," have long practiced this dubious principle of hierarchical tolerance—a Jesuitism of theory (for example, Catholicism and its essentialist hierarchy of "material" ethical essences). NP replaces these hierarchies with *a defense, in every case, of humans, and not of philosophy*—of humans taken "in-body" in their generic materiality and not "in-function" in their mathematical abstraction. Complementarily, it associates with this principle of the universal defense of humans qua generic subjects, a principle of minimizing the inevitable harm done to philosophy and to the modes of thought that are subordinate to it.

The empty-surface modern manifesto

The mathematical etiquette that authorizes our entry into the aristocratic society of scientists was at first geometrical (Plato). It is now, as all philosophers will tell you, principally topological. Badiou reprises the ideal of philosophical planification, hoping thereby to break with the effects of circularity. But he combines it with another ideal, that of torsion, which reunites or effects a passage from one plane of knowledge to another. What wisdom from this Platonizing philosopher who spends his time organizing, segmenting and ordering the past—that is to say, what we already know! Always this terrible memory of philosophy, this culture of the tradition that covets knowledge produced by others. It is rape and plunder, surplus-value and profit. Like Plato, but with less poetry and ambiguity, more unflinching than him, Badiou is a man of planes or levels of reality, differences and gaps, autonomous strata or "layers" one might say more abstractly or topologically, places and emplacements, just as Deleuze is a man of surfaces. Certainly, the planifier limits himself to three planes as opposed to the schizoanalyst's thousand, but this difference matters little, at most making for squabbles between disciples. It is a "modern" ideal, that of the surface in painting, of topology and the empty set, of the stratification of instances, of the trenchant nakedness of the manifesto as militant weapon. There is the Cartesian planification of "meditations" (to which Badiou sometimes has recourse), the Leibnizian planification of "mirrors," the multiplication of surfaces in Deleuze—it is a philosophical and hierarchical image of reality that agrees with the corpuscular spirit of every philosophy that cleaves to the "macroscopic" spirit. The ideal of ontological planification, such as Heidegger perceives it in the Moderns up to Nietzsche and his will to power, undergoes an inflection with the Hegelian and Marxist heritage of "instances" and "spheres." This modern ideal inscribes thought upon immobile ground, gives it a foundation, an architecture and a proof of its power. Ultimately, even in Nietzsche and Deleuze, it is a matter of thinking in "corpuscles," and of confusing the microscopics proper to philosophy (micro-philosophy) with the authentic quantum-theoretical inspiration and its undulatory aspect (which is oceanic rather than architec-tural). Badiou knows only the modern etiquette of mathematics, that is to say the void and the surface. In the same manner as the artistic "Supports/Surfaces" movement, we can imagine a philosophical "Void/Surface" movement. Needless to say, the affect of OV and that of NP are very much opposed: in one we have the desert and aridity, in the other, an overdetermined baroque of styles, interfering fluxes, and the swarming of conceptual particles.

Planifying and counting, Plato and Mao

We all know Badiou's mania for counting events of every order on the fingers of a single hand. He who celebrates the Cantorian multiple of multiples, begins modestly (often for others) with rarity and with a small number of philosophers, of revolutionary historical sequences, of poetic truths, of generic procedures. The two manifestos (and we await more, at the convenience of the philosophical conjuncture), the three degrees or stages of his construction, the two founders of Christianity, Jesus and Paul. But of course! Aside from the Platonic planification, this is the other secret of Badiouism: the Taoist enumeration, the three joys, the seven perfumes, the ten immortals, etc.—everything that could occupy a place (if a little forced) in Plato's transcendental arithmetic. The Badiouic universe is deployed vertically, through a staged superposition of scales, as in Chinese paintings: first, the good materialist of the mathematical earth, then men rebaptized as "subjects," and finally the skies of philosophy, the celestial hierarchy. This staging is what remains of the Marxist topography of instances, taken to pieces, and the Platonic edifice of philosophy, in which he rediscovers a sense for the hierarchical construction of regions of objects—the all, surveyed from afar, but nostalgically, by a Chinese encyclopedist.

Why only four truth procedures?—a frequent objection. To which we shall add: is a procedure generic from the start, or does every discipline have to *become* so? This extremely restrictive limitation and this rarity of actuality are indeed in the anti-democratic, even aristocratic, style. Of course, throughout, at every level (lower, middling, higher) there are exceptions, the elect of the Idea. A rarefied atmosphere, the atmosphere of the ascetic void. Even revolutionary history is rare; only the blissful multiple is inconsistent and cannot be enumerated. We find ourselves in a desert that we tramp through without surveying it, without flowing over it like Deleuze's desire; an arid country where it is difficult to breathe. Just as aristocratic communism declares itself against parliamentiarism-pétainism—truly a very narrow adversary given what is at stake, a disproportionate dualism between Maoism and pétainism. This is what explains the Nietzschean style of greatness, of great politics, of the great Heideggerian thinker, an epoch of greatness that philosophers fantasize about, and which here comes back onto the scene.

To pass from one stage of the edifice to the other, one needs an ascensional "line," which Plato formalized geometrically. As for Badiou, he develops a "meta-ontological" escalator—the famous "torsion" that permits an elevation that is smooth, but is also a leap. Which opposes him all the more to NP, with its baroque-style collision of philosophical and scientific instances, all thrown into a collider or a matrix as practices of a *non-standard philosophy*. Straight-up vertical, and thus "celestial," planification constitutes the major, properly philosophical activity of Badiou, the greatest planifier since Plato. The latter brought order to and between knowledges, arranging in strata and in "lineages" all anterior, pre-philosophical, religious, mathematical, physical, sociological knowledge. Badiou also limits philosophical action to the arrangement (one upon another, beside yet others) of the knowledges of his time, according to a topological hierarchy. Plato revisited via Dao and Mao rather than Aristotle, a combination at once *conservative and mandarin in spirit*. The Great Helmsman of philosophy leads an empty yoke ("chariot") that allows him to cross the famous "pass" so as to avoid "philosophical disasters." Needless to say, NP refuses the notion that philosophy should be a relatively formal, empty and sterile activity of the encyclopedic ordering and mastering of knowledges acquired from elsewhere outside of philosophy. If OV borrows its planification not from Marxism but from essentially statist communism, with its re-education and its necessary organizational violence, NP borrows its idea from the Marxist practice of the transformation of the situation of humans in the world. This alone suffices to explain many incompatibilities. Not to mention the differences in theoretical technology (which we shall detail below) in a corpus that is extremely limited but sufficient.

"Declaring" atheism: A precipitate usage of Platonism

In Badiou, Platonism, which already had a certain vocation to the ordering of reality, has clearly become planification. It has thus become what it was: authoritarian, a Platonism of the axiomatic "declaration" made on the basis of historical and cultural facts; facts which are then, moreover, deemed to be "fables," and put in parenthesis. The materialist decision, with no foundation other than that of declaring the Christ-event a fable—does this, for example, suffice for we-the-humans? Are we to satisfy ourselves with a "declaration," and a universal political program made for the new global intellectual, of the Saint Paul type—or are we faithful-in-the-last-instance to the kerygma or to the oraxioms that this supposed fable contains? Unless the christic "fable" is a kind of modelization, this amounts to once more returning religion to the realm of illusion, rather than treating it experimentally and for a new thought. One of the consequences of the primacy of philosophy over all knowledge is the elimination of the "presence" of other non-subtractive "philosophies," and, in general, of religiosity, however necessary it is to philosophical transcendence. A dramatic and theoretically simplistic decision that refuses to treat the religious, at minimum, as material or symptom; a decidedly devastating philosophy. To vanquish the religious, one must take it a little more seriously than a fable, or risk a truly vulgar atheism. Rather than the traditional unitary division between religion and/or philosophy, between fable and truth, there is a *unilateral duality* that inverts the terms of the division, and that must be rethought afresh.

Is not the theory of truth as "event" too voluntarist, lacking any real foundation? How does a mere "declaration" (even that of a "confession of faith") suffice, without a less formal—that is to say an a priori and material—axiom (an oraxiom)? We need the a priori of faith as the human power that receives and gives the fable, and thus the access to religion as symptom and then as model, if we are to succeed in destroying the beliefs that encompass faith. Faith—that is to say, fidelity— is doubtless confessed through declarations, but cannot be resolved entirely into them (an ideology of the priest); nor does it come "afterwards" (a theory of mastery). Always the aftermath of the declaration, of nomination, of decision—is not this the philosophy of the Master, the effect or the causality of decision? The problem is that of knowledge, or indeed the fable, and how they could serve as a support, or a springboard; but here they are too brutally suspended or invalidated, when they could have served as material and as symptom to transform with a less absolute but no less radical organon. Religion-fiction, this is what we can best do, in parallel reducing the religion of the Church to being its modelization.

Moreover, in the present context, the subject seems less an organon than a passive subject, so that the only master is Badiou himself, who has precipitately suspended knowledge and proclaimed his truth. In any case, he is a militant and contemplative, rather than a practical, materialist. Is truth a hole or a void (which so recalls the philosophical circle), or a process? The hole is the contemplative object *par excellence*, that into which we fall, but then the Idea that it reflects *raises us up through subtraction*—always the philosophical balance. The process is not that of the subject, but that of the material and the subject together—it is a practical and material labor, not just a labor that is subjective and transformative of the subject. There is a worldly or philosophical materiality of the subject, and it is this that is transformed, not only the subject's declarations and perseverance.

The elevator of the idea as intellectual descender

Complaining about the situation of philosophy, as all the most creative philosophers do, ends up engendering its own lassitude. It is we ourselves who have ceded too much to an anti-media obsession, one that should have brought into effect a science of philosophy, rather than, as in Badiou, a philosophical reaction that ends up profiting the media. We must take a more nuanced approach if do not wish to share the same mediocrity that we accuse the situation of. In a sense, it may be that philosophy only gets what it deserves and what it is capable of. From the point of view of production, our time, like any other, does not lack talents—even, to count on one hand à la Badiou, two or three philosophical geniuses. From the point of view of the distribution of philosophy to the greatest number and of its consumption, on the other hand, the situation is more complex. One can justifiably complain of the use made of philosophy in the mediatico-democratic regime. Antique philosophy and its wisdom, for example, is become the new opium of the people. Is not this a form of detestation of the people, an anti-theoretical regression taking itself for the mission of the intellectual? So much so that the intellectual demi-monde, which always used to include a certain number of philosophers on the margins of the ideological cyclone, has itself dissolved bit by bit into this cyclone. From now on it will be professional philosophers alone who, for reasons of academic normalization and media audience, form this demi-monde. At its highest extremity, it touches the "world" or philosophy, determined currently by thinkers like Badiou or Marion. At its other extremity, it touches the third-world that is henceforth that of intellectuals, the media fourth-world, even. And both put their admittedly real talents at the service of public and private money. Shall we also "planify," then—establishing a hierarchy of orders of philosophical greatness? A planification, let us say, that parodies Plato's and Badiou's, but that brings to light the fact that the motor that drives planification hooks up the philosophical elevator of the Idea to the intellectual descender of the media. Just so we understand: to rise and to fall is almost the same thing for all philosophers... Thus, they also live in the undulatory, but most of them try not to think about it.

Philosophy cut in two or delayed

Philosophy "under condition"—not the conditions of possibility for philosophy, but more exactly the condition of its exercise and its validity. For it is presupposed that there is philosophy, that its nature is known once and for all, but that its functioning is not totally free or spontaneous; that it is either badly normed or badly organized, and that, consequently, it must be limited by or filled with truths that it itself does not produce. Is this enough to avoid a positivism in the usage of science? Must we not posit all the same, at least in a Platonic form, the question of the right *of* and perhaps the right *to* philosophy, as Derrida does? Otherwise, the risk (among others) is that we see return the duality of ontological substance, and an empty formalism proper to philosophical ends. Philosophy no longer acts, it forfeits all action in the world apart from the guardianship of active or militant instances; it is a flag that we wave in the void. Badiou the writer, mathematician and militant recalls—at the last moment—that philosophy exists, and that it may well be necessary to assure him his position as ideal exception and as master of master-thinkers. To make it retreat as far as possible before the generic truths, and then before the transcendental of the world, to the point of a rupture where every necessity is ready to abandon it—here is an ethic of the guardian of the lighthouse or the watchtower. The whole "Aristotelian" substance of philosophy drains away, it is emptied, and all that remains is an envelope, a holey, despoiled sack used as a makeshift banner. Badiou brings philosophy to its last breath, threatening it with complete extinction, only to save it at the last moment by virtue of his proclamation. He creates a new formalism proper to philosophy, being the companion of a materialism that cannot totally break with it. Since philosophy is a question of pulsation, of periodic oscillation, it periodically tends towards zero-substance after periods of repletion, as if it had to digest its excesses of eating and drinking. There was the Socratic void, and now there is the Badiouic void. What is defined here as materialism does not go all the way to materiality, but limits it with a residual idealism: it is precisely a "dialectical" materialism.

Another distribution is possible between non-positional materiality and non-dialectical (or instead, "algebraic") formalism. To extend materiality to all of philosophy, one must consider that its putting under condition is underdetermining, or touches precisely on its intimate materiality, but does not condemn it to a formal void. And since it is a matter of avoiding a positive determination, NP limits determination to an *underdetermination* through the generic Last Instance.

Materialism is a philosophy at once anticipated qua materialism and delayed qua idealism. It is typical of OV (we will attend to the specular problems of doubling and scission that ensue) to delay explicit philosophy for as long as possible (in a manner other than that of deconstruction, through the void), all the while anticipating it, in dissimulated manner, as a basis or fundamental thesis. At first one admires its radicality, but it must be recognized that, by definition, founding itself only on the "transcending" that it isolates—on mathematics as pure decision—it presents itself (at least) as the most absolute, the most apparently consequential ontology in the history of philosophy. Its ambition is to escape from the hesitations of philosophy through the ontology of science (mathematical and then logical) alone. But (this is our whole thesis) this radicality is a dissimulated usage of the virtues of philosophy, from which Badiou deduces a trait that he ends up honoring *in extremis* and at the lowest possible cost. The ruse of materialist reason lies in this anticipated decision, whose idealist aspect is ferociously deferred, and which conceals itself in the attempt to excise ontology from philosophy and to make of the former an absolute knowledge. It fails to provide the scientific determination of philosophy that NP seeks, for its part, for all domains of the latter. OV reserves this determination for ontology alone—a half-solution that does justice neither to science nor to philosophy. However, we do not wish to say that the enterprise is lost—on the contrary, it is wholly successful qua philosophical. It is one more philosophy... and thus one more conservation. From our point of view, it remains within the molar usage of mathematical, logical and philosophical thought, with all the traditional finalities that each implies and that each prides itself on, seeking to impose it upon the others. But it does not succeed in making use of the means, beginning with suspending their own finalities. As always, the philosopher would be Nietzschean, would practice all genres as ideal knowledges (writer, artist, priest, mathematician, etc.), rather than dedicating himself to one that he would invent. He brushes up against them philosophically, rather than treating them as mere models with which to finally invent something else. And then he resorts to a torsion that he charges with resolving all problems. Doubtless one has need of a sort of universal means. NP also has its "fundamental" means or productive force—it is

quantum superposition in its generic usage. But precisely, here is
the means to finally exit from philosophy as self-encompassing
(PSP), by trying to create a new genre. The most complex
duality is not that between mathematics and philosophy, nor
even that (already less specular) between quantum thought and
philosophy. Even the latter must be oriented toward that of the
generic and the philosophical, which succeeds in bringing these
dualities to the state of a "unilateral complementarity"—none
other than NP.

Thus, a suspension and reappraisal of the old narcissistic
disciplines, necessitating the invention of an *apparatus of generic
thought—that is to say, a thought that is non-scientific and
non-philosophical*, in the sense that it makes use of science and
philosophy only as means—quantum means without quantum
finality, philosophical means without philosophical finality. Let
us understand that a philosophy split in two by the immixture
of mathematics, but by the same token merely delayed in its
return to glory, is not our affair. A means-without-end is not
a delayed finality, but, to be exact, one reconstructed with the
means as mere model. It is true that, since Kant, the problem
of philosophers has been to delay the coming of philosophy,
which they thus suppose to be already present; to work at
differing or distending it from itself, from its unity with itself.
Deconstructions are certainly no exception to this treatment,
but neither is Badiou, any more than one should prematurely
oppose him to these practices, when in fact he consummates
the separation of science from philosophy, purifying the latter
from all mixture. Certainly, as well as differences in context

(mathematical versus language), in technique (planification versus dissemination, purification against contamination), and in politics (the Stranger excluded by the State versus the diasporic Stranger), he adds a materialist and atheist, rather than Judaic, deconstruction. These differences suffice for philosophers with a propensity toward becoming-intellectual, but scarcely more than that. NP is a practice *of* philosophy, not a philosophical taking of sides and thus *inside* philosophy.

What remains of philosophy?

Amputated from ontology, itself identified with mathematics, what remains of philosophy, if not that vague and academic definition of a thinking that maintains with the events of its times "a relation of thought such that this relation is universalizable"? This minimal and trivial program belongs effectively to every philosophy, and suggests an impoverished and reduced reflexivity, somehow deprived of the principal object that it has always been recognized for: Being, and thus also beings, either Presence or the supposed correlation of ontological Difference. This decision, which truncates the body of philosophy, has no meaning, however, except under three conditions that limit its signification:

1 That ontology should be safeguarded, albeit outside of philosophy and by virtue of science. A few words on what fulfills or realizes this ontology: Badiou reprises Platonism only to modify or modulate it with two or

three other traditions. These include: (a) the Cantorian
auto-reflection of mathematics, which he substitutes
for "reflection," for "consciousness" and for "difference,"
and which is the type of thinking proper to a scientific
knowledge which he claims satisfies ontology (if
not philosophy itself, which will think with its own
categorial reflexivity), and which must suffice for the
logos of mathematical Being. Traditional philosophical
self-reflection is thus amputated and relayed by this
quasi-thing-oriented [*quasi-chosal*] knowledge. In
NP, the distribution is made otherwise: no longer
the foreclosure of self-reflection by mathematical
knowledge, with, beyond it, a return to reflection, but
the vision-in-One or force-(of)-thought as non-reflective
superposition-(of)-self, with reflection serving only as
material; (b) The residue of the (not Marxist but Maoist)
primacy of the dialectic over materialism. Set theory
constitutes an ontologico-scientific quasi-genesis; it
supposes a fund-of-multiple for the theory of the event
and the undecidable. The primacy (hierarchical, or
through domination) of the dialectic over materialism
is given here as primacy of transcendence over
immanence. In NP, this type of problem would lead
instead to the "primacy"—to the prior-to-priority
without-hierarchy—of materialism over the dialectic,
that is to say of the real-One-of-the-last-instance
over thought as superposed identity of science and
philosophy.

2   That ontology, better still, should be at once
    independent of philosophy and yet also simply detached
    from philosophy by a Cantorian cut, as the subtracted
    or separated part of the old pre-modern image of
    philosophy ("presence"). This scientific cut into the
    Aristotelian body of philosophy takes the form of a
    Cantorian rather than a Galilean revolution. But the
    philosophical, from our point of view, is always barred
    or affected by the scientific—except, to be exact, for a
    subject who would be a pure "practical" mathematician.
    Thus, it maintains a fundamentally ambiguous status,
    being outside-philosophy only because it continues
    to be immediately retained by the latter. In general,
    Badiou refuses to theorize this type of conditioning
    or passage, whereas for NP it is obligatory to examine
    it, under the name of "unilateral complementarity," in
    which one must include subtraction and its supposed
    independence. Moreover, the refusal to take into
    account (even in the smallest way) acts and not only
    states, is doubtless a relic of the severing of thought
    from all language. Under the name of "ontology," the
    immediate identity of mathematics and philosophy is
    equivalent to a no less immediate detachment of the
    ontological itself; and here the problem becomes still
    more crucial. Philosophy, already deprived of this and
    that being (regional ontologies), now sees fundamental
    ontology subtracted from it as well—a subtraction,
    however, that continues to suppose the omnivalidity and

presence of the philosophical, by way of a topological torsion. We do not think that philosophy can escape abstraction by advocating the difference between topological distinctions and predicative distinctions. Like all recent "contemporary" thinkers, but in the modern mode of the unique scientific cut (from this point of view, he represents a classical regression in relation to Marx, who overdetermined the cut) and no longer in the postmodern mode of the multiple cut (Foucault), Badiou pursues the deadening and ascetic work of subtraction, the ascetic Ideal of transcendence which sub-tracts itself and sur-treats or sur-tracts itself in its doublets.

3 That the philosophical itself, better still, should return from the beyond of the Cantorian cut, first of all, under the mask of the theory of the undecidable Event and of decision. As practice, and in its most comprehensive invariant, the philosophical seems to us to be defined precisely by the couple or the dyad of the undecidable and decision. The real ("Being"), itself undecidable, contains adumbrated, latent, virtual decisions, at the edge of Being or of the undecidable, which can only be actualized and realized through the supplement of a decision. In the implicit state, the decision is detained in the undecidable, and only a supplementary decision can extract it from that state of undecidability and reverse it, tip it over into a second state of the undecidable—or

inscribe it in this state. Now, this philosophical invariant undoubtedly finds its context reversed here (the real is decision and not undecidable, and the event is undecidable). But it is limited as soon as it is attributed to the event alone, when in fact it conditions philosophical ontology, that is to say "ontological Difference" or "presence," from within. The immediate identity of the mathematical and the ontological cannot but leave the philosophical thinned-out, in "plan(e) view," one might say, in the form of the theory of the Event—as if the philosophical had been, under the pretext of modernity, cut in two, split between Being and Event. We thus understand that objectivism—its affect of the "in itself"—having been exercised a first time in regard to Being, is exercised a second time in regard to the Event, and that the latter must in turn be detached from the philosophical body.

What else could remain to philosophy, thus deprived of torso and limbs, other than the head—reflection with no proper content, the contemplation of categorial "compossibility" deprived even of the ideal of totalization or of the encyclopedic? The reception and inventory of generic truths—this really is a minimal program. And what reception? If it is passive, and transforms neither philosophy nor truths, then what is the point? The true classical work of philosophy will have all been done previously, before it entered onto the scene and into its glory; philosophy itself would now remain as a mere mirror, or an empty tomb. Ultimately the "return" is the only true concrete activity of philosophy (as always, no doubt); but philosophers generally at least put it to some trouble, making it pay the price for its return. Subsequently Badiou will claim to have filled the hiatus between ontology and philosophy with the transcendental logic of worlds, but in fact this only deepens and confirms it, by way of exactly the same procedure.

We now understand why a "philosophy" so impoverished and dismembered (but dismembered otherwise than was Dionysus) needs to be defended and celebrated by "manifestos"... Measured against this slaughterhouse logic, it is non-philosophy that is the true defender of philosophy. It is true that Badiou began his first "manifesto" with the puerile operation of an enumeration on one hand of "current philosophies." Just to reassure him, we will not cut off his fingers, for how would he do arithmetic then? Indeed, he has taken one more step in modernity, that is to say in philosophy. But if modernity is still a matter of philosophy, then he also took one less step in the philosophy of our conjuncture. A step that is also not a retreat, a "step back." Retreating only as far as Plato, he did not retreat to that which preceded Plato's mathematical planification—the *physis* of the first pre-philosophers, who were physicists. But this is hardly the problem; when will we finally, rather than a hundred idle steps in the lobby of philosophy, take one step *on* philosophy as upon a new continent—or a new wave?

What remains to man as subject?

Let us admit the well-foundedness of mathematical ontology (we shall elaborate its genealogy in the next chapter). What consequences can be drawn from this? It seems to us that OV here meets with the same difficulty as deconstruction: their inspiration is, despite everything, still religious, for reasons of hyper-philosophical transcendence, even if Badiou fiercely denies this. This is nothing serious; what is a serious matter is the refusal to recognize it through a sufficient analysis of all philosophy. How could a thinking (of) the *absolute* Other—either as Idea and Good à la Plato, or as affect of the Absolute à la Judaism for Derrida—be possible without appeal to an onto-theo-logical Other? Plato and Levinas, the two inspirations, obviously knew nothing of these modern negations, which testify to a rather miserable atheism that confuses its personal beliefs with the objective conditions of philosophy (conditions which, themselves, do not forgive, and only wait to betray the thinker). Decidedly, vulgar atheism is a secondary position of thought, fit only for badly reformed believers and "bad-very-bad" faith. A divine inspiration is, however, accorded to the atheist-yet-Platonist materialist who plays at atheist boasting; just as Judaic inspiration is accorded to the deconstructor who believes, sometimes naively, that it is enough for him to "deconstruct" his philosophical beliefs in order to distance himself from or to marginalize faith. OV supposes, as one might expect, the dissolution of the One or of man as individual, replacing it with the subject as determined by the (here ontologico-mathematical)

Other that condemns the subject to an evental dispersion or to a transitory identity. One may well ask, moreover, whether OV remains in the neighborhood of Levinas—whether this Other-(of the)-void is not wholly *intelligible* here (can there perhaps be no Jewish mathematician in the way in which there can be a Jewish philosopher?) The mathematical decision, the void itself—are they not, then, *causa sui* and auto-nominated? But here again, how can the pure transcending affect itself, and what would there be to affect? On the one hand, man is definitively lacking, or is but a mode of the void, which is possible only on condition of re-introducing him surreptitiously by way of philosophy—by way of the philosopher-mathematician, who risks (effacing himself in this very gesture, as we have said) the mathematical decision. And consequently it would be better, it seems to us, rather than this unrecognized division of man into a (rare) subject and an shamefaced hybrid philosopher-mathematician, to extract the essence of man from his avatars and from these games of transcendence, identifying it with the radical generic (not absolute) immanence that alone can "found" transcendence. The philosopher-mathematician or militant must come to pass in the place where man is, rather than the other way around. On the other hand, it is difficult to see how the ontologico-mathematical void can affect Presence (even if only to exclude it) if not precisely by supposing this problem to be resolved—that is to say, by supposing the void, after all, to be correlated and relative to Presence, which is the solution of unitary appearance, that of all forms of transcendence.

To these problems is attached another: who subtracts? The

philosopher, who returns to us one more time, at once identical without mediation to the scientist (if not to the auto-effacing mediation of the decision) and distinct from him. Science is no longer the support nor the springboard of decision. Decision is now identified as a sort of flattening of itself onto already-constituted scientific knowledge, so that we believe that we discover, immediately legible and visible in constituted knowledge itself, ontological rationality or the laws of being. But once more, according to an antique schema, only a meta-ontologist (the descendant of the philosopher) can perceive the meaning of what happens in this ontology blind to itself, in this logos as mute as calculation. The silent ontology that is mathematics has need of the most traditional supplement, that of the philosopher as *deus ex machina*.

The generic man-subject and the particulate ego

The true "subject" of NP as generic science, who cannot be discovered as philosophical, is thus discoverable (but not identifiable properly speaking) as subject *transformed* into generic man, rather than as mathematics-dependent "humanity function" (Badiou). The generic is quantum-theoretically complexified in relation to a simple "materialist" separation from philosophy. It is an undulatory, superposed or interfering lived, which accompanies particles of egological origin. Again, this definition is too simplified in all respects. *The man-subject of philosophy is reversed into the generic subject-man*; this is the displacement into-prior-to-priority of man as generic, implying immanently the displacement of the transcendent ego, which is no longer at the heart of the lived but on its margins. It must be admitted that generic man is not deprived of all subjectivity, at least qua lived. But one is obliged to separate the generic neutralized lived from the subject proper (subject-existent-Stranger), who is unilateralized, particulate or unifacialized. The proletariat is a concept of the subject of history; but in order to be transformed as bound variable of (quantum) science and of philosophy of history, he becomes objective-generic (but not, for all that, philosophical). He is humanized but desubjectivized, in the sense that he loses his principal predicates of consciousness and reflection. A prior-to-first passivity.

Similarly, psychoanalysis would have had to have introduced quantum algebra rather than the pure mathematics of the "letter" (Lacan) into the philosophy of the imaginary in order to have become a generic science. The "subject" of the psychoanalytic act is divided up transcendently between the analyst and the "analysand" (a still-idealist *lapsus* in which media psychoanalysis remains engulfed, that present participle attesting to the transcendent tendency to the act or the decision of the subject). The old Cartesian subject has been transformed with the help of the analyst, who submits it to the alterity of the signifier, a structuralist equivalent of quantum theory—the "subject of science" (Lacan) still too close to the transcendental cogito. Psychologico-mathematical psychoanalysis is overdetermination through alterity, as the science of the imaginary of the "analysand" subject; it remains a still imaginary-objective science.

The notion of generic psychoanalysis as unified theory of Judaism and individual psychology is obtained, this time, through their superposition; by producing a generic subject that complexifies the analysand subject with the analyst, who thus form together a *generic subject* for psychoanalysis, a *unilateral complementarity*. Thus is transformed the concept of *auto-*analysis, which came down to refitting spontaneous psychology or philosophy, the Cartesian cogito included. We obtain what should have been the scientific but not formal concept of analysis—which is, in fact, generic analysis or dualysis. In trans-cendent psychoanalysis, alterity was thought as hole or lack in transcendence, and thus as a doubled hole or a doublet of lack, distributed between two individuals, the analyst advocating the immanence of the cure as act. Now, he can "only be authorized by himself" on condition that he should thus be, in another sense, the analysand, or that he should be the indiscernible unity defined by a unique state vector—the *unified analyst* being the generic man who cannot be distributed between two individuals with heterogeneous functions. Analyst and analyzed both participate in the *generic analysis that is distributed according to the law of unilateral duality*. The two heterogeneous functions must be superposed or added together, their wave function distributed according to the principle of unilateral complemen-tarity. If the analyst introduces immanence by superposition of the analytic process rather than that of the "act," it is qua prior-to-priority—the two parts or the two knowledges representing, in their duality, the imaginary to be transformed. There is no analysand, nothing but the analyzed-without-analysis who is the Last Instance or the generic subject-man, a function of knowledges to be added together. The generic analyst or the non-analyst is a bound variable, a function of the psychological imaginary complicated with the function of the variable, let us say the Judaic variable, put into quantum position.

3

Old and new relations between science and philosophy

Philosophy placed under rigorous invention

If there is philosophy, alongside many other things, it is its affirmation or claim, left to itself and unbridled, in Badiou's work in particular, that characterizes today's intellectual conjuncture. The present conjuncture of NP is not what Badiou says it is—its excess after its death-by-media; Badiou himself also thinks within the couplet media philosophy/pure philosophy. He belongs to the same configuration of an evaluation of philosophy as superior doxa. He knows only how to oscillate between its death and its survival, its excess and its rarity, its plural and its singularity, its deconstruction and its absolutization—as if it could only exist, and only exist as claimant, in the enclosed compound of its harassing dualities. Precisely, the rare new propositions that appear, Badiou's included, are still partly repetitions and defenses of doctrinal positions, reprises of tradition or "returns." Just as the discourse of the Church constitutes a "development of dogma" through which it survives, so the variations of philosophical discourse constitute the development of a tradition upon which it supports itself. But if the dogma is the "cumulative" treasury, the philosophical tradition is an academic treasury that is largely sterile, where almost everything is lost (or is conserved only by the university), or is destined for reproduction. And it is this basic sterility, which Badiou would celebrate and glorify, that for us poses a new problem.

In this context, his excellent formula "putting philosophy under condition" must be taken up, but in a profoundly modified form. Its apparent modesty in fact signifies an exacerbation of philosophy by the very means of its subtraction from knowledge. From the negative that it becomes through subtraction, to the presence of this condition that only serves to delay the return of philosophy, we transform it positively but against all positivism, placing it under a condition that is determining-in-the-last-instance. Once Truth is posited, Badiou is interested only in the modalities of philosophy. And there are either too many or not enough secondary modalities—but hardly any (or none at all) that attain the global status of the philosophizing whose kernel he admits, in reducing it to the minimum still thinkable. This is a restoration in relation to Heidegger, and a good many other thinkers who were interested in its mechanism (for it does have a mechanism). There is nothing here that could really change the course or the practice of thought. To liberal and general reaction responds this purified communist reaction. Difficult to find, once this similarity is unmasked, any more interest or possibility of invention in one than in the other.

In a direct address to planification and the foundational spirit, Badiou suggests that Deleuze retreated before an objection to which he did not respond—namely, that set theory is more powerful and more fundamental than the logic of inclusive disjunction. Maybe he is right, but from our point of view, this type of objection condemns him to confess his philosophical desire for foundation or, at the limit, for auto-foundation. It truly takes a philosopher to seek supposedly the most powerful mathematics, the most foundational, as if traditional philosophy had lost its true aim. Whereas Deleuze was just an engineer, a philosopher of *bricolage*, and one who brought it to an unequalled point—unfortunately also bequeathing to certain of his disciples the ideal of a pop-philosophy that is indeed one of the low water marks of philosophical activity. Philosophies are often collections of bric-a-brac, encumbered with a little of everything, but it took the genius of Deleuze to render his own acceptable, even desirable. Badiou, on the contrary, makes us breath the keen and Cartesian air of scarcely inhabited heights. He immediately proceeds with his "decluttering," separating himself from all cumbrous and useless things. His topological planification deals with the old conceptual furniture even worse than did the "plane of immanence" (Deleuze). But here again it is the effect of a "modern" cut, this time artificial, that rejects philosophical work on and with authors, in texts curiously dubbed "meditations." The Cartesian spiritual unity of demonstration and meditation is broken up by a planification, an enumeration of planes.

But even if they are artisanal montages, bricolages even, philosophies all possess a transcendental core, in various forms. The heart of philosophy lies in the transcendental, which in reality is a double doublet (empirico-transcendental, transcendental-real). This ternary, almost quadripartite division is the pivot of the non-philosophical critique of sufficiency. To separate the two doublets is without doubt to conserve the lesser, in the form of a materialist transcendental; but it is also to absolutize the second and to deprive it of a transcendental, to make it into an inert superstructure. It is a great temptation to refer the transcendental to the logical, or else to history, and to reserve for philosophy the rational, architectonic higher-level functions. No doubt Badiou treats admirably each of these levels, clearing passageways or corridors from one to the other by way of his topological torsion. But this dismembering of philosophy into three instances, like so many autonomous planes of reality— ontological, logico-transcendental, philosophical—belongs to a "separatism" that is ancient, and which has become largely unintelligible or unusable for contemporaries who, when they invent, prefer multiple variables or parameters, their matrixial and complex combination, either quantum or generic, to the ancient rigid practice of planification. This separatism is for Badiou the essential activity of the philosopher, who has in some way lost his substance or his grand possessions, and has become a refugee in a passably haughty solitude.

NP risks another ambition, declaring it in full awareness of the difficulty of its realization: *to place philosophy under the complex condition of the science that under-determines it generically as rigorous invention.* Here again we require, for the deregulations, fictions and utopias to which we aspire, necessary principles of order, scientific models, a new conception of creation and the displacement of parameters. Under the proliferation of the titles of non-philosophy, anti-philosophy, post-philosophy, without-philosophy, even pop-philosophy, certain negative conditions of our project have already been fulfilled by others, certain of its codes identified. It remains to whoever wishes to do so, to propose new decisions. It is not necessarily a matter of new "great philosophies" with a hegemonic vision, but at least of texts that could be called, globally, "non-standard." By definition, we do not entirely know what to expect of ourselves.

This essay might be read as a *project* of the exercise of philo-fiction on Badiou; it would allow us to verify the operatory character of NP on what presents itself as a defense of standard philosophy. We would have to imagine for an instant a quantum-theorist rather than a mathematician Badiou, a contemporary rather than a modern Badiou, one in the lineage of Bohr and Heisenberg rather than Plato. This would be an exercise in "quantification" understood in the non-logical sense of quantum practice or dualysis: a quantification that is not quantitative, but which conserves, as *Non-Standard Philosophy* demonstrates, an ultimate link with physics by way of a quantum of generic action. His thought would be, for us, a body or a part of nature, a new philosophical object upon which we would carry out an experiment or provoke a reaction. The matrix of NP thus receives a new version or a new formula that generalizes and neutralizes this philosophy generically. It would be a matter of making Badiou's thought pass from the primacy of the mathematical and the void to the primacy of physics, by taking account of the philosophical gesture intricated in and with this primacy. Badiou as philosopher means the subtraction of the Multiple or of the void of Being, from presence as One. But our formula would be (using his own language) subtraction of the One-in-One as radical immanence obtained by quantum superposition, from presence as Being. Which is not to say the overdetermination of the Multiple by the count-as-one or by the metaphysical One (precisely what Badiou disallowed for his count), but the quantum superposition of the One-in-One and the Multiple. The major statement of set-theoretical materialism would then be the object of a philo-fiction, supposing a major transformation of the content of its terms through their insertion and forcing into a generic matrix of immanence—the abandonment of transcendent planification. The true reduction of the One is not achieved via Cantorian mathematical means with the help of an ontology, but via its fusion or its superposition in-One with the Multiple, which then rejects the count-as-one in a corpuscular state. The change of context is radical from the mathematical to the physical context: we pass from a set-theoretical logos to an algebraic "logos" which leaves behind a certain dogmatism, and which, always mathematical in a sense, leaves behind, thanks to its generic form, the authoritarian materialist position, just as mathematics left behind its encompassing character. Materiality is substituted for materialism, the algebraic syntaxes of idempotence and of the imaginary number for set-theoretical syntax. The whole operation is a transformation, via generic formalization, of Badiou's philosophical statement mathematics = ontology. The old Cantorian multiple would then be irreflexive, a lived wave without torsional unity; and the count-as-one a particulate object. For this to take place, the Multiple must no longer be defined mathematically, in an immediate identity with Being, but must belong to an algebraically defined ontology. Thus, the One and the Multiple alike change their mathematical and above all their "ontological" sense, as they are brought together under the custody of the One-in-One or immanence. There must, of course, be new axioms to invent on the basis of the Badiou-symptom and its material, symptoms which are his philosophy.

Science: Critical purification or transformation of philosophy?

There is an apparent similarity, a deceptive proximity, between truth and transcendental illusion. Kant (K) and Fichte (F) both denounce it, but nevertheless do so using the means of philosophy. They seek a science of philosophy, but at the same time step back into the philosophical circle. Badiou also denounces it, separating in trenchant manner philosophy = ontology from presence *and* mathematics = the void, but still has to register the return of philosophy. NP seeks in a science and its (immanental) "ontology" the dissolution of illusion, this time philosophical or dialectical illusion in the form of doublets of immanental origin—an illusion that is therefore more than merely "transcendental." Seen globally, and in a first approximation, both undertake the same combat against error, presence and representation, the same delimitation through the usage of truth or truths. We begin both within truth (which is the "negative" cause of illusion) and within error (which, then, is its positive cause), an error that we denounce progressively. In any case, we must limit the religio-philosophical circle, and for this reason take aid from science. Even the elementary logic of identity is necessary (F), albeit of limited import. In still very global terms, this is a struggle undertaken by a "science-subject." But given this global basis, many differences can be identified.

Badiou believes himself protected from the return of philosophy in its Aristotelian and Heideggerian configuration (the principal adversary) by mathematics = the void; the void reassures with its apparent absoluteness. If ontology is that of the logic of the principle of identity, the result is more ambiguous; thus, K/F must extricate themselves *dialectically* from presence. The problem is therefore a question of means, and at this point science enters onto the scene, but a "science-subject" *that proves that science can affect or initiate philosophy* because, inversely, philosophy believes that it masters the science-subject through its position as subject. The science-subject (in general) is either the critical-negative factor of transcendental dialectical illusion

(K/F), or the critical-positive factor of philosophical appearance (OV and NP).

Do we begin in the mixture of illusion and truth, like Kant, Fichte and Descartes? No doubt, but what type of mixture? In OV, it is uncertain whether the mixture has any reality or consistency. For K/F, it is an appearance or an amphiboly of which the All (the identification of the phenomenon and the thing in itself) is the cause and the beneficiary. For NP (as for OV), the appearance is not without reality, but neither is it total, and destructible only for theological reasons (K/F), or is only so via a unilateral identification—for the algebraic identi-fication of subject with science, or rather their superposition, is at the same time that which has already saved us (virtually, but not yet actually or effectively) from confusion. We begin with amphiboly, but it is unilateral: *the means of salvation are apparently the same as those of the loss*; the kernel of truth is immediately pre-empted over the all or torn from philosophy. We do not fight against the total illusion of philosophy on the basis of the latter, but under the determining condition of the science-subject.

NP avails itself from the outset of the kernel of truth encom-passed by appearance, paying no mind to the philosophical objections that inevitably present themselves. The scientific stance is from the outset constructible axiomatically, at the very heart of philosophical appearance, contrary to Fichte and Descartes but like Kant, for whom the logic of truth comes before that of transcendental appearance (to think otherwise would be to suppose that one still takes the philosophical All as starting point). The science-subject as kernel of truth permits one to combat and transform the appearance, in which it is the negative cause that does nothing.

The purification of philosophy by mathematics is not its science but just a struggle against presence, against the negative aspect of appearance, decided and rejected in one go as error or "disaster," rather than vanquished stage by stage (K, F, and NP). How does Badiou show that void mathematics has an effect on philosophy? Not only is mathematics the text of ontology, it is the meta-ontology that takes the place of the subject in the science-subject. But meta-ontology testifies to the primacy of philosophy in its work on itself—it takes science in hand and places it in its service; whereas in NP, it is science that appropriates the subject that philosophy believes belongs to it alone. Science is not merely at the service of the critique of philosophy, but also, and first of all, at the service of the science of philosophy. Either science is at the service of philosophy's critique of itself—thus Badiou's conservatism, which sees itself as a conservation; or philosophy is at the service of science (the science of philosophy), and has immanent critical effects. Thus, the denunciation of illusion, of the very existence of illusion, is ambiguous: K/F and Badiou place it at the ultimate service of philosophy, so that *illusion is still perceived through philosophy itself, as if it were to be its mistress one last time—in this case, we get materialism.* They cannot accept that the illusion is total, since they "are" philosophers; whereas for NP it is the *whole* of philosophy that must be denounced, and precisely not *as* philosophy, but as positive immanental illusion that could be or could become the object of a science—a very different position. In NP, philo-sophical illusion is denounced and perceived prior-to-priority (and thus not exclusively) by the science-subject that initiates the appearance of philosophy and limits it. As in Derrida's Judaism, there is a positivity here that is not philosophical: the science that conceals the divine or monotheism, and that initiates philosophy extra-territorially. NP therefore rediscovers a certain exteriority of deconstruction, but rediscovers it as the transformation of philosophy. Badiou is the conservator for an epoch of intellectual recession that he consequently fights all the more strongly and violently, bracing himself against the fortress "philosophy." NP denounces illusion *in immanent exteriority or through the exteriority of real immanence*, whereas OV continues to pledge itself to philosophy.

But if the science-subject is "ontology" torn from philosophy, how can it constitute itself without a meta-ontology? The new quantum partition passes between micro- and macro-; a displacement that annuls the power of general logic and the logic of identity/contradiction. We pass from the tradi-tional couplet logic/philosophy to the couplet transcendence/ immanence, from void atomism to undulatory immanence. *The notion of transcendental illusion has no purchase here; it is an immanental appearance.* Transcendental dialectic and the theme of presence would now be ill-fitting in any case: presence is linked to the primacy of transcendence, whence the importance of the theory of elements as immanence and transcendence to exit this problematic. Modern science, not reified in a theory, avoids speaking of representation in general, or of presence, and characterizes the problem or the stakes otherwise—for example, with the distinction between classical logic (which is atomist) and quantum logic. It displaces the mechanism of illusion. The latter is no longer transcendental, but immanental, a confusion of philosophy with real immanence. *Modern science and its contemporary usage force us to think otherwise, rather than re-confirming one more time our love for eternal, perennial or stellar philosophy.* Badiou's whole labor in the history of philosophy consists in rediscovering his positions give or take minor deviations, and it is a most weak transformation of philosophy. This is just the classical labor of philosophy—to find oneself in it for better or for worse, rather than considering it with respect and neutrality as an object to be penetrated, as all science does, and transformed. Strictly speaking, he accomplishes the philosophical side of the work, that is to say the work of transforming systems by "leftwinging" [*gauchissant*] or twisting them in a partisan manner (see his Deleuze); but he explains nothing scientifically with regard to these systems. He determines nothing, contenting himself with placing them under condition (that is to say, under the subtraction or purification of philosophy) without axiomatising, deducing and experimenting with a new knowledge of them as (for example) non-epistemological universals. For him, something is always lacking, something that philosophers have not done, that they forgot to do or did badly. It is true that his philosophy, rather distinctively, reserves the possibility of failure in the midst of an exalted heroism, but from this to speak of "disaster"... Always the falling of stars, the falling of the Philosophical Star...

All of these problems stem from the fact that philosophy imposes itself dogmatically as the inevitable starting point. But why would a scientific procedure not be a good possible starting point, on condition that an individual or a collective agree on it and identify with it or take the scientific stance, that of the science-subject? *As humans, we allow ourselves to be subjectivated by science. Certainly, it is miraculous, like the discovery of a new principle, but this permits us to free ourselves from a certain philosophical yoke.* There are two types of human or two human "becomings": those that identify themselves with the All under various imaginary forms, and those that identify themselves with a scientific procedure and think according to it. Thus, there are two subjects, the All-subject or the philosopher-religious type, and the Procedure-subject or the philosopher-scientific type. Any subject whatsoever can be identified in these two ways, and is transformed by this insertion. This is to recognize the specificity of the (at least virtual) scientific stance for and among humans, not only that of the current philosophical stance as the ideal image of man. We need not be definitively and eternally confronted with the objection of the philosophical and/or epistemological circle; this problem can be dealt with through the series of operations permitted by the generic science-subject. On condition that we recognize in the scientist a subject implicated by the procedure, and not just an exterior agent manipulating procedures, there is a virtual or generic scientific *stance*. Science is not a rupture in relation to or within philosophy; there is a duality of stances. Science is indeed radical autonomy, and has no need of being epistemologically reduced, and yet it necessitates the aid of philosophy *if* one wishes to adjoin thought to it—and one always does adjoin thought to it, for it is at least philosophiz*able*. The only problem is, inversely, that the All then monopolizes the science-subject or the generic human lived that is prior-to-first. Philosophy and the science-subject (without being yet the science of philosophy) thus form an amphibological appearance from philosophy's point of view: it posits *their unity as amphiboly or appearance of unity of the lived*. In a sense, the problem is not very well posed, or can be misunderstood, if one says that the subject comes from philosophy or is furnished by the latter, that there is a redistribution of the supposedly total sphere of the lived—as if one admitted the starting point in the philosophical all, which is but an immanental unilateral appearance. It is thus, precisely, a solution that is still too close to that of K/F and that of Badiou.

The dogmatism of anti-philosophy

The originary epistemo-logical difference between sciences and philosophies is never a simple difference. It is intrinsically specular, and is wrought of the doubled fabric of transcendence. Even Deleuze does not arrive at a simple radical, but remains, in spite of everything, with a full body as Moebian self-doubling. Badiou begins, like every philosopher, with Parmenides, and with mathematical entities and ontology. They are no longer simply "epistemological" since they are voided of their reciprocal reflection that would reconstitute a superior transcendental instance. All the same, the identity of ontology and mathematics is inscribed in a pre-existing materialist position that is the sign that philosophy is present. NP's solution is different: we also believe that it is necessary to know what is philosophy and what is science; but we begin from a generic stance, with its dose of skepticism, not a dogmatic one. We do not support ourselves on a dogmatic *unilateral cut* between two terms, philosophy and ontology, as if science could break its alliance with philosophy with one swing of the axe, all the while identifying science with its ontological part, and making this duality appear after the fact. Instead, our stance is subtended by a *prior-to-first duality or unilateral complementarity* which reserves an ambiguity of relations between the second term and the first. This is the difference between the unitary cut, where unity remains in the background and returns to science in the constitutive form of a meta-ontology, and unilateral duality, where philosophy does not return in constitutive manner.

For the materialist reading of mathematics and its axioms supposes an a priori cut: Badiou slices into the body of philosophy with a materialist decision, which means that mathematics is not really autonomous, since then it would have no need in principle of materialism and ontology. A science given and posited as absolute paradigm (a philosophical gesture), cutting itself off from philosophy, obviously lays itself open to being taken up again by the latter as constitutive of the real—which is why the quantum physics we utilize *is not a new philosophical paradigm, but a de-finalized means in the service of the transformation of philosophy*. NP allows the algebraic element its specific reality, recognizes its operativity, but recognizes *explicitly* that this is possible on condition of thinking science as implying a certain overthrowing of philosophy as ultimate reference, and at the same time acquiring a quasi-transcendental but irreflexive nature or function. Badiou apparently has no need to posit science as overthrowing of philosophy; he posits science directly against philosophy, which it divides unilaterally, in exteriority and not in interiority. Now, this refusal of philosophy flattens out the One and the Multiple from the start, by using a particular positive scientific body of knowledge, making of it a "foundation." He is then obliged, if he wishes to surpass this limited positivity of set theory, to reread (with the help of meta-ontology) all of the mathematics he was deprived of by the materialist cut. He metaphorizes ontologically a particular body of knowledge, and transforms it directly into essence, according it the status of an essence, combining positive particularity and meta-ontological generality on the basis of this materialist cut. He proceeds with a displacement onto a terrain other than the transcendental linguistic and auto-encompassing transcendental One. A displacement through the attribution of Being to the cut or of the real to materialist scission rather than to the transcendental One. But even in this case, there must be a displacement here, in the form of the materialist presupposition admitted against the style of the presupposition. As soon as an irreducible presupposition is admitted, one changes terrain purely and simply in relation to philosophizability—which does not take long to return, in semi-unconscious manner, since it was not recognized.

The formal theory of philosophy as preparation for its science

A theory that we shall call the formal theory of philosophy is nevertheless necessary as preparation of the object for its generic science. It must pass from the claim or from the phenomenon to being, being constituted in its *corpuscular object-being in view of its transformation into its particle-being*. If we suppose that philosophy can be a scientific object, equally we admit that it is enveloped in appearances and in lures. It is therefore necessary to have at our disposal a criteria of identification for that object, even for the "greatest" of authors. Doubtless, it has become a sophistic discourse, all-purpose, vulgar, all over the media, most often among babbling intellectuals. Badiou brings together the most extreme claim to philosophical authenticity and its demonstration through the most brilliant oeuvre, and yet one hesitates to say that he gives rise to "a philosophy."

Quantum thinking gives rise internally and externally to innumerable philosophical interpretations. There was an affinity in principle between it and philosophy that was to favor its transcendental interpretation. Quantum thought has many midwives, but only one birth, in many phases. Quantum thought allows itself *on first appearances* to be interpreted according to a transcendental schema, three sources being necessary for this: (1) Most importantly, the quantum of action that corresponds to the transcendental operator that traces and determines the limits of the objects of quantum thinking, and makes it possible as science; (2) The classical corpuscular physics that corresponds to the empirical domain to be described and normed (predicted), and which presents itself as symptom; (3) The elevation of the wave function or the state vector to the function of a priori legislation of the empirical domain. Quantum thought finds its theoretical basis with the association, admitted as necessary, of two paradigms more or less indifferent to each other (wave and particle) in a new figure, that of indivisible complementarity, if not quantum correlation, and which is also emitted in "packets." It is remarkable that the wave should already be in itself a transcendental movement, the gesture of a surpassing of itself in itself, and of auto-delimitation (the transcendental wave creates an appearance—that of its horizontal displacement), and that to better describe (not mathematize) this undulatory intuition, it should suffice to see emerge the future transcendental interpretations of quantum thought, in parallel with a philosophy of the wave or the vibration (Nietzsche and Deleuze) which, obviously, does not manage to do full justice to it.

Strictly speaking, the "quantum of action" plays a quasi-transcendental role: it differentiates and unites two phenomena by fixing the minimal but necessary measure that is exchanged between them. And from this point of view, it does not legislate over classical physics, but is the principle that allows the submission of this empirical domain of the classical to the a priori or undulatory domain. In a certain sense, quantum theory is the physics of the Newtonian world, itself too imprecise and *general* (and partly of the world of relativity, too)—just as NP would be the science of the transcendental, the science of the world constituted by philosophy. For in the transcendental interpretation, specular doublings and redoublings are inevitable. Whence the task of NP: to explain and to limit through explanation, to transform the transcendental, to *pass* into the sphere of the immanental. We no longer work on things or on in-itselfs, on metaphysical semanticism, but on already-scientific representations. They are points of view, perspectives and interpretations, languages also, which turn around unknowns=X and which are our ordinary; all that serves to embed and locate that which we conserve of the mathematical apparatus.

The philosopher living in the milieu of the "foundational" ideal and absorbed by it can only rid himself of philosophical foundation if he places it and finds it elsewhere—for example, in the mathematics and set theory to which he attributes this power of founding, or that he solicits with this hope. But the non-philosopher renounces wholly all foundation, renouncing it not only for philosophy but also for science. He accepts that he works on a science that is contingent, in the sense that it reduces as far as possible the foundational pertinence of science. The essential point is that it should be a knowledge that cannot be furnished by philosophy. Not only must we abandon the foundational function of philosophy; we must abandon foundation everywhere as an ancient ideal of thought. But this does not mean to say that we abandon only an ontical foundation, and conserve the eidetic absolute. However, rather than auto-presenting itself as philosophy or as sufficient practice without theoretically elucidating its essence, NP as science supposes a formal theory of philosophy that identifies its invariant and varied transcendental essence. Rather than a formal mathematics, in NP we have a formal theory of philosophy, of its essence independently of every object or aim or given of the world, but which is not yet its science as object. This is why it is important to verify whether a theory is or is not philosophical (that is to say, transcendental) in essence, beneath its philosophical appearance and its external aims. What is more, this identification is not a description of appearances, but falls already under the determining condition of the principles of a generic science. It is important to identify a philosopher expressly despite his auto-sufficiency, his auto-nominations or his masks. This is not to force an open door, or to say the same thing as him, since this preparatory theory of the object or the phenomenon, its preparation as macroscopic object, depends upon the science of that object itself. The formal theory of philosophy as transcendental is necessarily a simple half-inductive half-deductive theory. It seems precisely to be an auto-theory of philosophy—unless NP intervenes as negative condition of this theory, which will then no longer be sufficient, but will be placed under condition.

Non-philosophy is not a meta-philosophy

NP is not a meta-theory. It is a non-theoreticist theory—which, obviously, is not the negation of theory. In its early texts, it still retains aspects of meta-theory, since those texts remained in the grip of philosophical authority. But NP precisely reduces meta-human statements in general. This error often crops up, because philosophers think that theory is simply given, and that one can then pass to the second degree. Whereas exactly the inverse is the case: philosophy is a complex object or a doubling, *already* a second degree and thus already a meta-philosophy. Every philosophy is the meta-philosophy of another, or of itself, because it functions as that which supplies its own rules, to a greater or lesser extent. It is a matter of a specular doublet, whether one considers it on the plane of a concept, of a problematic, or globally. NP, on the contrary, is a simplified state of philosophy, a non-metaphilosophy, an effort at reducing reduplication. But obviously, attaining the simple takes a lot of work, and necessitates the deployment of a complex thought. This poses a general problem of repetition—of its contestation, of the weakening of its philosophical omnipotence or its sufficiency. It is no longer a matter of philosophy's famous surpassing of itself, a gesture that forms the explicit motor of almost all nineteenth-century thought and a good deal of what remains of speculation in twentieth-century thought.

Neither is NP itself a formal theory of philosophy seeking to defend the latter without caring for its *object-being*, or contenting itself with confirming it and defending it rather than defending subjects against it. NP has always had a consistent philosophical object, and has never dreamt of a pure theory of philosophy that would make of it that flattest of things, a formal truth. What distinguishes us from formal set-theoreticism is a physical semi-formalism. Mathematics in OV affixes its status to other procedures, and this approach results in a formal devastation: philosophy leaves behind it a scorched earth, as it retreats after its defeat in the face of the Real rather than in the face of reality. It engenders only more formal theories without object, including a philosophy emptied yet a little more of its substance. That philosophy should lose progressively its non-specific objects to the sciences is inevitable, and perhaps desirable; but it does not lose its so-called "fundamental" or traditional objects, the transcendentals and the categories, and above all the syntax of its transcendental gesture. All of that endures, however much it may stale into the worst kind of doxa. It is these objects that we need a science of. In seeking to eliminate them from philosophy in favor of an empty category of truth and even of logic, in seeking to eliminate them from the science of philosophy, one supposes that mathematics has a direct effect on philosophy, as if mathematics projected itself into philosophy. A mirror effect, as if philosophy were very nearly the image of mathematics, or its twin. One can never make a science of philosophy with mathematics alone, even if one empties it of all substance. One ends up with nothing more than a materialist formalism of empty axiomatic writing—an exercise in writing, the novel of set theory. This philosophy is not only a philosophy "of" the void, it is really at the limit of void as Being without object or "reality," and as a result is all the more reduced to an activity of pure proclamation. Badiou's purism replaces the object of theory with the representation of presentation. But the object is not necessarily (as he implicitly supposes) that which gives phenomenological or ecstatic distance; it can be given immanently, indirectly and semi-ecstatically. This is the whole interest of the wave function, in which the object is not given in the ontologico-Aristotelian mode, nor in the Platonic mode of the Idea. To take as the basis of existence a theory (set theory) or a knowledge that is formal and without object, is to flatten existence onto the void. Even art, politics and ethics become rarefied when they are forced into this Procrustean bed of an inhuman multiple. It is not "crude" materialism, here less than ever—it is very sophisticated, intellectually respectable, even. But it is flat and bereft of interest—the mirror-image of philosophico-transcendental idealism, which is also a formal theory of auto-exposition. In both cases, the formal theory interprets the world, but does not transform it. Thus, even set-theoreticism falls prey to Marx's condemnation. The generic can no longer be philosophical, but must be practical, in the sense of a real (not contemplative or formal) transformation of events. This is the principle of a real, *marxisant* critique of the contemplative exaltation of the materialist void. It exalts only its own formal intelligence, at the risk of an authoritarian sterility... And of boredom...

4

Matrices and principles

A deduction of the set-theoretical thesis

The foundational thesis *mathematics = ontology* is not itself scientific, but makes use of science and of philosophy. It was intended to be scientific, but it remains merely a materialist thesis. This would only be possible, only rigorous (or undogmatic, in any case) if it were deduced as a theorem, and thus under conditions more complex than those of set-theoretical ontology, conditions that engaged with thought as a quasi-physics of philosophy. As things stand, it is in fact a decision or an "axiom"—a materialist thesis wherein materialism tries to think itself, a thesis that therefore seeks not only to be "ontological" but also claims to absorb the totality of ontology and to deprive philosophy of it— whence its violent character of slicing and tearing away. A thesis or an axiom cannot stand alone, or claim to found itself. It must be aided, if not mediated, by another, by a philosophy. Certainly, philosophy does indeed intervene here, or is requisitioned under the auspices of its traditional ontological bedrock; but the element capable of generating Badiou's major thesis must be more and otherwise complex than the thesis itself. For what can the bloc of set-theoreticism (sets + ontology) achieve, of itself? Either it is an "intricated" unity, philosophically self-intricated, that claims to found itself and to operate the act of subtraction— an act that conceals another, more pure, philosophical-style auto-foundation, but which does not know itself as such or is not announced explicitly; or else it requires a relatively detached meta-ontological act of being-posited, an explicit intervention of positing. Badiou as materialist tries to flatten one onto the other the object posited and the idealist act of positing. The difference in the two cases is the difference between the implicit and the explicit, but that makes no difference to the decisionist or arbitrary structure at work here.

From our point of view, to leave behind this arbitrariness, one must deduce the thesis or the equation on the basis of a more "powerful" machine than it (no longer conflating the power of the philosophical absolute and the power of the non-philo-sophical radical, which is the power of a certain weakness). This other machine is necessary to avoid the tautology, the vicious circle, that is at work in every philosophy, and must be of the following type, at once generic and quantum-style—what we call the generic matrix: *in it, the fusion or unity of the Set and of Being is not philosophically overdetermined by Being, but under-determined by the Set; it is thus not at all determined in the form of an (explicit or implicit) auto-foundation.* Grasped at a certain level of generality, the matrix is the same, but is specified into two versions, the philosophical and the generic. Consequently, it reorganizes otherwise Badiou's distribution; another partition is necessary that would not be that of the philosophical division (that is, of the meta-ontological subject itself), but that of the generic sharing-out or distribution of the subject (as we have seen, between subject as Last Instance and subject-Stranger operator or clone of the philosophical subject). In other words, this fusion is underdetermined by the generic Subject, and occasionally determined by the clone-subject or Stranger. Under this condition, set-theoretical ontology is a theorem, rather than a thesis. Set theory and ontology being transformed at the same time, the Set gives rise to a generic theory that transforms set theory profoundly, and the real of Being gives rise to the immanence of the One through quantum superposition.

Types of the generic: By hybridization, selection, and matrix

The generic by hybridization is its weakest and most abstract form: it designates a median generality obtained by a certain leveling. Badiou's generic marks the distinction, we might say, between Aristotelian disciplines and Platonizing procedures, which have an ontological vocation or are intermediaries, mediations "toward" philosophy. Entirely according to his transcendent set-theoretical technique, he makes it a factor of aristocratic selection and planification. This factor, which Plato puts to work in the sciences, is transposed into the form of the four generic truths. Whence, in the contemporary epoch of the interdisciplinarity (indiscipline, even) of knowledge, a strange scent of nostalgia. Finally, against unthought and empirical hybridization, non-conceptualized hybridization, against the aristocratic selection directly opposed to democratic hybridization (both corpuscular in spirit), NP is another concept that is realized by means of the quantum matrix, superposition and non-commutativity. It is a matrixial and generic (and thus non-dialectical) conception of knowledges thrown into this collider to produce new knowledges.

It is urgent that we avail ourselves of the generic stance as the becoming of all knowledges, as "good hybridization." NP sets itself in another relation of generic becoming in relation to a certain, more expanded, range of disciplines— science, politics, art, erotics no doubt, but also technology, religion, and philosophy itself. The classical knowledges have to become generic, but we shall continue to address them using their classical names. We call generic matrix this chamber of immanent transformation, this collider of knowledges forced to exit from the orbit of philosophy by themselves, with the recognized aid of philosophy (explicitly assumed, but reduced in its turn). Certain disciplines are not necessarily and from the start "generic" rather than ontologico-empirical; but are susceptible to producing generic knowledge. This generic knowledge is not given a priori. How to address, from the point of view of their universality, love, art, politics, religion or technics, which are not knowledges in the rigorous sense? "Truth procedures" is Badiou's formulation, a fine formulation indeed. But rather than the couplet of the generic, or truths, *and* the philosophical, NP uses "stances of truth," which is less technical, more human and perhaps broader, *and which, above all, can also encompass philosophy*, since the problem is that of their all arriving at the generic, a trait that is not given them from the start. Whence a new partition, a redistribution between philosophy's supposing of itself in itself (PSP), and the generic becoming that can encompass even philosophy, as non-philosophy, and perhaps even mathematics. They are stances of knowing that are capable of generic truth, and of distinguishing themselves from the couplet of positive sciences and spontaneous (transcendental) philosophy that they cut up according to another type of division.

The principles of OV and NP

To clarify the problem, we shall refer to two versions of the matrix, that of OV and that of NP, exhibiting firstly their two or three "principles" (variables, ultimately), science and philosophy, which are both contained in each of the matrices. More than ever, we are at the heart of decision.

The matrix used by Badiou rests upon two principles, which are thus not immediately visible as objects or themes: the *principle of planification* and the *principle of torsion*. Their unity implies a third principle still less visible and more secondary, that of *repetition* at the limit of presence. The two first principles are comparable to the two principles of quantum thought that we use in the new or "non-standard" form of NP: the *principle of superposition* and the *principle of non-commutativity*. The principles of OV are predominantly philosophical, but are effectuated with regard to and in science (set theory). Those of NP are predominantly scientific, but are effectuated within philosophy. Judging from immediate appearances, OV seems more "scientific" than NP because it speaks of scarcely anything else but science, and NP speaks of scarcely anything else but philosophy. In the real relation, the inverse is the case: NP is more fundamentally scientific, because it begins with a certain primacy (prior-to-priority) of quantum thought over its philosophical object, to which are attributed only "hermeneutic" functions. OV places science in the service of philosophy; NP places philosophy in the service of a thinking-science. This clarifies a certain ambiguity with regard to the two theories.

Planification is the philosophical form corresponding to quantum superposition. They are two principles of "identity" in the rough sense of the word—identification not of objects, but of knowledges or disciplines. Planification is a veritable identification in the sense that it depends on its objects, which are of a corpuscular type, albeit intellectual corpuscles or particles belonging to a classical logic of identity. Superposition, on the other hand, is an identification in an apparent sense, since it does not apply to corpuscular objects but to those undulatory phenomena that science and philosophy will necessarily be. "Quantification" (in the broad sense of the quantum-theoretical operation) also obliges one to consider apparently given phenomena as macroscopic objects, as undulatory phenomena— which is to say, simultaneously, as particulate phenomena.

Torsion is the topological principle that "corresponds" to the quantum non-commutativity of the inverse products of two variables (here, the two disciplines). Moebian torsion is, at best, the non-commutativity of two directions of the plane. These directions, treated as variables brought into the matrix, give rise to equal inverse products, thus contradicting Heisenberg's Uncertainty Principle. It is thus a simply formal non-commu- tativity, which leaves as is the contents of variables (that is, of disciplines). On the other hand, the algebraic or quantum non-commutativity of inverse products of variables in the matrix has a material and not merely a formal sense. This principle is more individuating than topological torsion: it defines the uncertainty that (according to Heisenberg) makes it so that the two properties under consideration are not attributable to the same object but to two distinct objects.

We now see the profound opposition between OV and NP, between a topology of concepts and a physics of concepts. It remains to render more precisely the fact that each of these matrices has two principles, accompanied by a dimension of unilaterality, but which are in OV ultimately reversible and mechanical, and in NP ultimately or in-the-last-instance irreversible, submitted solely to a complementarity or a duality that can correctly be called "unilateral." Take Badiou's key formula: to put philosophy under the scientific condition; and take the key formula of non-philosophy: to put philosophy under the scientific condition that is determining-in-the-last-instance. The resemblance between the formulae is only apparent. The first defends philosophy in its essence, limiting only its bad usage or its ontological overambition; the second takes aim at the essence of philosophy, and sees in its overambition and its travesties only inessential conjunctural phenomena that are permitted in principle by the structure of the philosophical act. The first believes that the present existence of philosophy is essential and suffices; the second is not satisfied with this existence, along with all the various benefits that it procures for its glorifiers.

The backlash of the condition

Finally, a third principle that Badiou considers as secondary but which we shall later give its proper status by showing how OV tries to dissimulate it. The two matrices establish a backlash or a repetition of the condition, a backlash of philosophy on science or "inversely" of science on philosophy or on a still more complex instance (that of their conjugation). This backlash signifies that philosophy, or indeed quantum theory, always returns a second time—for this is a theoretical machine, a matrix with three places: the two variables of science and philosophy that one supposes canonically conjugable, and a third which is the return *as factor* of one or the other of these variables. As Kierkegaard says of the paradox, for it to be intelligible and complete, its "condition" must be given. For our part, we say that it must either be given as the philosophy that completes OV by closing it, or operated as the quantum theory that completes NP (without closing it, this time). Here we find a whole den of nuances and appearances that will be explicated little by little.

The matrix of OV is predominantly philosophical, that of NP predominantly scientific, but this is still very general. OV posits a meta-ontological relation to science, a backlash or return of philosophy as "first instance," one might say. NP posits a backlash or return of science as "prior-to-first" instance, or as last instance for philosophy. OV marches forth one more time for philosophy, as if it had to protest or "manifest" for philosophy, which is already every possible manifestation; as if the actuality of existence had to be repeated, like a weakness that does not allow itself to be recognized. NP defends science by showing the transformation that it inflicts upon philosophy, but does not take up arms on science's behalf, since science knows its weakness and must, if not repeat itself, at least strike back or be "resumed." The condition, which is thus always that of "repetition," is in the first case implicit or invisible: it is a prejudice of philosophy to imagine itself so self-evident that it would never dream of interrogating its deepest mechanism. It has already returned, and the backlash is natural and uninterrogated. In the other case, it is explicit, the backlash of science being nothing less than evident, and demanding to be operated. Whence a paradox: OV does not seem to repeat philosophy or dissimulate its repetition, whereas NP explicitly repeats the scientific condition. Now, it will be shown that the inapparent revival of philosophy in OV is a true repetition, because its principle is a transcendent decision; whereas the apparent repetition of science in NP is rather what we shall call a resumption, because of its principle, the undulatory superposition of immanence.

The two matrices and their variables

1   The initial kernel of OV, to put it very schematically, is an "identification" of science and philosophy, but neither of them in their totality: it is an identification of the mathematical part of science or the axiomatized-set-theoretical part of mathematics, and philosophy—but a philosophy cut or divided up, reduced to ontology. We must take seriously the equation that renders inseparable set theory and ontology, because this initial "identification" of disciplinary variables is fundamental for understanding the matrix of OV and planification. Marx gave its general formulation: the fusion of the forces of production and the relations of production, FP and RP (under RP). There is a fusion of the Set as FP and of Being as RP. This flattening is a simple identification and an ontological translation of set-theoreticism, and here we see at work the flatness of materialist equalities. On the contrary, the quantum version of this equation posits its members as superposable and as non-commutative, but not as planes. NP substitutes for the mathematical equation mathematics = ontology their fusion or superposition.

2   But this equation taken as is, is particularly inert,
and supposes an agent capable of deciphering and
activating it—meta-ontology as compromise between
the materialist set-theoretical position and the necessity
of a philosophical-type intervention. This is possible
given that the doxa "philosophy" has been cut off from
its properly philosophical part, which remains unused,
kept in reserve, but can therefore be employed for more
operatory purposes. The ensuing labor must consist in
decomposing meta-ontology itself, and finding within
it with a new strata—logic and its quasi-transcendental
character. Therefore, there cannot but be a return or a
repetition of the philosophy that has been suspended,
even if Badiou's strategy consists in repressing it for as
long as possible and emphasizing the maximal force of
mathematics upon the traditional terrains of philosophy.
The mathematician gives himself the right to enter into
the depths of philosophy's hunting grounds—that is to
say, those of the subject. But nothing has fundamentally
changed in the global matrix—the initial equation is
valid only insofar as it is completed by a functioning that
returns upon it and determines it. However necessary a
part of it remains, philosophy is exsanguinated or purified.
One might ask oneself whether Badiou, in playing this
game, does not lose on both tables: he stifles philosophy,
voiding it of all substance—brings it to the edge of its own
void and requires it only (albeit noisily) as a witness or
stance (even probably after *Logics of Worlds*). And what

is more, he always has need of it, as his matrix implies,
and thus conjugates idealism with materialism. He gives
himself philosophy only to plan(e) it, like a sort of matter
or passive condition, within a formal horizon that he must
admit at the end of his enterprise. Everything seems to be
ultimately determined by mathematics, but this is only
an appearance; in fact, everything is overdetermined by
the generality of Being, or better still by the category of
Truth. He respects the most general matrix, but gives it
an ultimate philosophical sense. Doubtless a purified or
threadbare idealism, gnawed at from within and without
by mathematics and logic, but still absolutely necessary
and formally encompassing the all—a kind of shamefaced
philosophism.

His matrix therefore only functions with what we must in the first
instance and very imperfectly call an "identity," a "repetition" and
an "overdetermination." Supposing (1) an immediate identification
of the two members, whence a forgotten and floating remainder of
ontologico-linguistic concepts linked to the aspect (passed over
in silence) of their "translation"; (2) an aspect from which is
surreptitiously pared off the meta-ontological act; (3) and which
is animated from beyond by philosophy and its transcendence.
Obviously these planes are meticulously cut out, purified of
language, not inserted into their linguistic conditions of existence
(which are absolutely refused); but they are linked mathematically
by the principle of torsion that is the keystone of them all (in
NP this keystone is *unilateral* complementarity). Whatever the

modalities of the solution may be, the category of Truth that makes for philosophy must have had a certain hold upon mathematics, or a relation to it. It is not a matter of a Marxian-Althusserian overdetermination, which remains conceptual and is modelled on mechanics, but that of a topological and processual means or descent, honoring Plato more than Marx.

Badiou is an idealist-materialist like Marx, but without giving himself the means to think in the Last Instance. For this requires another means capable of operating the generic. It requires quantum theory—physics, not mathematics. Only quantum theory and its principles can think a Last Instance that would be the superposition of mathematics and philosophy rather than their identification, and that would be non-commutable with their product (philosophy of quantum theory *versus* quantum theory of philosophy). Finally, Badiou reduces the philosophical to a simple kernel of mathematico-topological properties; and as to what remains, it becomes a harmless ornamental border of fictions. Even in this form it is difficult to accept this wager, the risk being that of suggesting that the whole edifice is itself a fiction—or a great myth?—which would, after all, be an honorable solution.

The materialist thesis and the generic chamber; closure and access

The materialist thesis plays the same role in philosophy as the experimental chamber, the theoretical chamber that we call generic: that of a closed or semi-closed site or framework within which one handles variables. We must interpret in this way the "problematic" in Marx and Althusser, and in particular the definition of the Last Instance as fusion of FP and RP under RP. Badiou posits as content of the materialist thesis the immediate identity of the Set and of Being, through a unilaterally oriented reading. He does not posit the problem of variables to be multiplied one by the other (philosophy or the concept cannot be interpreted as a mere set—or at least, this problem is not posed), but that of their immediate identity with a "final" primacy of the Set, and a meta-ontological remainder that will be necessary in its future role as a certain stratum of overdetermination. Ontology is reduced transparently to set-theoretical structures, and the thickness of Being vanishes but returns as meta-ontology or meta-materialism. Unilaterality is simple and goes from one term to the other: it passes between two terms. Badiou is unilaterally and mechanically a set-theorist in ontology: he does not return immediately from the latter to the former, but keeps meta-ontology in reserve and represses it until the last possible moment. Abstract mechanical unilaterality and meta-ontology go hand-in-hand.

In NP and its generic matrix, there is an inversion of the products of variables, but this takes place always in view of their non-commutativity. Unilaterality does not pass between two simple terms, but between four terms (or four occurrences, with an inversion of products). Meta-ontology would itself be that which interprets science, for quantum theory is necessarily in its turn a variable to be interpreted (contra Badiou's positivism)—so this is an inverted double reading. But then, does the reversed unilaterality disappear in favor of infinite reversibility? No, *because unilaterality is reaffirmed, this time definitively, but in a complex and no longer mechanical manner, by quantum theory—and yet this is not scientism or positivism.* This is the whole difference between scientistic, mechanical or philosophical unilaterality (which are all the same thing from our point of view) and the quantum unilaterality that destroys mechanistic materialism. For the quantum interpretation of philosophy-of-quantum-theory is itself a last unilateralization that confirms the prior-to-priority of quantum theory over philosophy. It is the same idea as that of the distinction between simple unilateral machines like Deleuze's and complex unilateral machines like generic matrices. We must no longer oppose unilateral machines to molecular machines, for the latter are also unilateral, but are mechanical or internal to philosophy. This is the general problem of molecular and materialist theses qua theses or philosophical framework-spaces of a macroscopic nature. The generic point of view makes use of philosophy without being detained in it, but by definitively unilateralizing it, completing it without closing it. It makes use of non-commutativity for variables within the chamber or the thesis, and makes use of superposition outside the thesis or the chamber. That is to say, it unilateralizes it and the subjective generically through its very interpretation. There is thus a great difference between a thinker of materiality and a materialist thinker.

In relation to these fundamental problems, we will distinguish between the Husserlian clause of the axiomatic closure of scientificity and our own clause of completion without closure; between the necessity of a scientific chamber that is complete but not closed and the nomological ideal of Husserl, who speaks of a theory as an "ideally closed totality" of formal laws unifying a "domain" of formal objects. The disjunction between a mathematicism universalizing its domain formally and the physicist experimentation upon philosophy without formally closing it, leaving it the function of a "hermeneutic" variable to interpret quantum theory, is here consummated in the generic conception. The latter reduces all science and perhaps mathematics itself; in any case, this type of generic chamber, in the neighborhood of man as generic subject, in view of procuring for this latter an access to sciences and to philosophy. It may be that the problem of the (non-psychological) access of humans to science and to philosophy proves ultimately to be more decisive for the latter than their sufficient and all-encompassing development. Badiou gives no quarter in his argumentation, and "forces" set-theoretical ontology and logic, differing beyond all deconstruction the return of philosophy, as if he also (but otherwise than Husserl, as the inverted materialist image of the latter's mathematical idealism) was fascinated by mathematicizing auto-formalization.

Repetition and resumption of prior-to-first passivity

The generic immanental and the materialist transcendental, how do they resemble each other, sometimes to the point of fooling one into confusing them with each other? In fact, science returns twice in Badiou, once as mathematics and then again as logic. But in both cases to fulfill the same function, that of a non-transformed object or *fixed plane*, not that of a theoretical means. These returns constitute a progression in the complexity of the staged construction (the planification), but not a return of science as subject, of the science-subject or the Last Instance; they do not arrive at the subject prior-to-priority; the return is instead that of the remainder of the philosophical subject as logico-transcendental. The logical transcendental gesture comes to be lodged in the initial gap left between philosophy and mathematics. Philosophy is not at first seen according to science, suspended by it or reduced to the state of a symptom; it anticipates itself as real, something that is possible with mathematics but not with quantum physics, since the latter marks the end of the primacy of mathematics at the moment when it is most intensively employed. This specular *chorismos* is conducive to doublings. To admit philosophy as a milieu is to make of it an *absolute, a priori position*, not a merely material symptom. In which case, it is not worth defending it, since one has already posited it absolutely— all efforts to defend it from then on are intra-philosophical, and demonstrate only that one has not understood what is in question, namely this very positing. On the contrary, we posit it from the outset as a symptom that is non-sufficient (without double transcendence). The more that philosophy is posited as actual and pertinent, the more its defense is of a warlike order. The more it is posited as symptom and not as in-itself, the more its defense is of the order of transformation and invention.

Badiou thinks in gaps that are too wide—between the empty category of Truth and set-theoretical practice, between the Idea of philosophy and the empirical and conjunctural modalities of its existence, between the communist Idea and pétaino-parliamentarism. This want of schematism or mediation, or of tools, at least, is conducive to excess and to deviations, to the impossibility of adjusting thought to reality. He does not retain Althusser's concern for correctness and adjustment. This is an effect of the planification that stratifies, cuts and slices exces-sively the planes of reality. The Platonic *chorismos* and its effects can be seen in the struggle between the Aristotelian initiatives of mediation. Philosophy is doubtless obliged to oscillate between *chorismos* and suture. But the question is whether another solution might not be possible, beyond these two and their eternal conflict.

Before *Logics of Worlds*, Badiou recognized the want of "mediation" in the dualism of Being and Event, of Sky and Earth (to indulge in a little *chinoiserie*), and tried to correct this, but by using exactly the same procedure. To generalize the problem, it is that of experimentation on two interacting bodies, mathematics and philosophy—upon which plane, at what level of generality, does it take place? Let us look again at the matrices. The philosophical mechanism puts into play two variables, and a function that repeats one of the variables. The absolute position that is philosophy, admitted from the outset as pertinent, is in reality a double transcendence, a doublet (either empirico- or logico-transcendental). But it is interpreted or decided by Badiou as having to be a materialist position that thus knows nothing of its deepest mechanism, the doublet, but that, by virtue of this doublet, closes itself upon itself. He therefore installs himself (this is his specific maneuver) in the space of the gap philosophy-without-ontology/set-theory-as-ontology; and then, since the gap is still too wide, he later inserts into it the transcendental schema of logic. Everything thus takes place in-between mathematics and philosophical transcendence. On one hand, they are identified in terms of the inseparability of the empty Set and Being. But on the other, philosophy, motivated by its residual or remaining part (ontology and transcendental logic having been removed) has not abandoned its absolute position, which has not been put in question, and thus returns upon the whole set of planes, empty and breathless. It is an extenuated phantom, an emptied-out and abstract body that comes back to remind those who do not have the ears to hear—science, art, politics and love—of the promise of ancient nuptials. The doublet is forgotten in this mechanism, and it is this forgetting that drives it, that prompts philosophy to widen the gap by making it believe that, in this way, it can close it. What best to do? Void philosophy of its entire substance, tear it out by tearing out the best of its objects, so as to keep more pure the disincarnated philosophical ideal? Or void it of its sufficiency, keeping its proper materiality without further conflating it with the objects that have been unduly attributed to it?

NP prepares an interaction between quantum theory and philosophy that must replace the hierarchical, idealist or materialist transcendental device. Quantum theory as superposition of passivity has the power of "resuming" itself, if not repeating itself, or of determining philosophy as symptom. It determines it not immediately but in-the-last-instance, which saves, despite its status as symptom, the reality *otherwise* in itself of the object "philosophy." This is not an idealist suspension that annihilates reality, but nor is this ultimate determination of the symptom a "disaster." Because of this resumption of immanence, science is in a quasi-transcendental position, and differentiates the two sides of quantum theory and philosophy. But precisely it is not a doubling of and in transcendence, as in philosophy (which is, therefore, spontaneously transcendental), but a twisting-without-torsion, immanent and without *chorismos*. NP is immanental, philosophy is transcendental. The immanental has traits in common with philosophy, but it is a resumption of science, not of philosophy. One can engender philosophy and generic NP on the basis of that basic structure that is the most general triangulation, tri-phase or tripod, of which NP gives the immanental example, philosophy the transcendental—partially generic and scientific in Badiou, idealist elsewhere.

In the generic matrix

The materiality of disciplinary variables

We shall no longer treat knowledges as sufficient essences, conceptualizable or idealized, as does epistemology. But neither shall we treat them as generic truths in themselves, as does Badiou. This would be to suppose that the generic is attached in privileged manner to certain empirical knowledges, and above all, it would be to overly rarefy interesting knowledges. The NP matrix presupposes in its functioning a generic *treatment* that is, if not already in operation, at least virtual, and which must be actualized. Disciplines here are considered as means for a knowledge to be produced, like variables of a system that will obey quantum principles under the generic. This is to reconstruct all knowledge as material production, as well as the theory of the means-of-knowing, which will no longer be a matter of faculties, but of developed knowledges; a better analysis of the material means as non-subsumable under philosophical finalities, but as capable of a minor or immanent finality that is their operativity and that is also a part of their materiality.

Each of these knowledges is reduced to its invariants under its own responsibility. In themselves, according to the quasi-physical model of NP, they are material particles that must be treated by quantum, algebraic means, not arithmetico-philosophical means; by means of matrices, not analysis and synthesis. This method of treatment of the multiplicities of knowledge replaces hybridization, which is a philosophical-style biunivocal combination. What is more, the quantum principles and the resumption of superposition are applied to complex objects irreducible to the forms of analysis and composition that are judgment and cognition (in Kant, for example). To perceive them as corpuscular, we must obviously be in the unilateral between-two of the corpuscular and the undulatory. If we consider the philosophical style according to criteria other than the labels it has made for itself, from the point of view of quantum theory, the notion of radical immanence has many models. There is a corpuscular model, whether it be immanent and transcendental, closed, individual, full of affectivity, in a finite and stationary circuit. And another model, undulatory but also complex, open, incomplete, transfinite or trans-stationary, or (as we say) oceano-stationary (as opposed to the *state* or the *system* in the quantum sense and to its own model of the terrestrial universe). These two models of thought are ordinarily mixed together in philosophy in inverse proportions, with the corpuscular dominating in the classical style. NP is thus a horizontal redistribution, rather than an inversion, of the relation of these two models, with a prior-to-priority of the undulatory over the corpuscular. Philosophy is not uniquely corpuscular, and non-philosophy is not uniquely undulatory, but there is an Undulatory or Quantum Turn "in" philosophy here—both in the ultimate substance of thought, which is the lived rather than affectivity, and in the way it is formulated, whether conceptual and rigid or fluid and flowing.

Knowledges close us in, harass us as cosmos or logos. An ethics of de-specialization against the excess of "specialization" does not, however, signify the ideal of ignorance, nor even the (Socratic) ideal of the recognition of one's own ignorance. It is a matter of subordinating knowledges that are already too corpus-cular, and whose finality is institutional (here also lies their being founded in the world, which Husserl quite rightly rejected) to another, generic relation. Beyond merely shaking up their usage, we mean to introduce into it the unexpected, uncertainty—a true indetermination. We shall treat knowledges validated within their order as elementary givens, received in aleatory manner and treatable in quantum terms; as philosophical-type means combined with means that are *otherwise* scientific or complex, that is to say generic—destined to become equal entities, floating, indeterminate philosophical variables, in which one can store philosophy. The latter is also, once more, taken to the level of a knowledge that receives a generic universality of presence without being universally powerful or sufficient. This statute of knowledges and of philosophy obliges us to seek a new type of order, against philosophical hierarchies—a necessary general de-suturing of knowledges and of philosophy, itself treatable as *a particular knowledge that accompanies all others (in memory of its ancient function) but that has the same status as them qua generic knowledge.* It must be admitted that there is an immanent finality of philosophy, one which is not transcendent doubling, and which can be combined with the immanent ends of other knowledges. Philosophy, also, is a variable in a matrix.

We cannot decide that there are generic knowledges on one side and then, on the other, a philosophy *of* the generic but which itself is not generic—a distinction that allows Badiou to safeguard philosophy and its privileges. In Badiou, the generic depends upon the privileging of the classical couplet mathematics/philosophy, which produces a set-theoretical generic. We oppose to this a generic matrix that has need of quantum physics and of philosophical reflexivity, but only as mere means. We propose another distribution: knowledges—including philosophy—must all become equal in the generic, while conserving their difference in disciplinary technique and materiality. But we do not know in advance why and if they will be as Badiou supposes and decides; we have to render them equal by way of a matrix, a matrixial chamber that transforms them into generic means. Our task is to produce these truths as such—they are not spontaneously given. This is the unified theory founded on the univocity of the generic, whereas Badiou's minimalist thesis admits a certain equivocity of the generic.

As to the privilege we seem to accord to quantum physics in our superposition or immanence, it is the symmetrical term of philosophical universality-as-means or variable. In both cases, it is a matter of reducing disciplines to the state of means-without-philosophical-finality, but, in doing so, of conceiving the specificity of their own operation that belongs to their materiality. Quantum theory is not the same as the generic, which we do not attribute either to any privileged knowledge nor to any one science; the generic is effectuated by quantum-and-philosophical means, but is a phenomenon that belongs only to humans, and draws from them its origin and its real possibility.

Quantware: The torsion of the imaginary number

Alongside the materiality of the generic matrix there is its quantware, the indivisible package of its syntax or of its way of thinking. Let us approach it from afar, starting with the relation between intellectuals and philosophers. The complaints of creators about the lack of philosophy in their times bears witness to a malaise whose broadest formula or whose a priori framework, we postulate, was given by Marx under the title "fusion of theory with the masses." To give it its full pertinence, it must be compared straight away with Parmenides' formula, which can be rephrased "fusion of Being and Thinking in the Same." They are homologous, and give rise to appearances certain of which affect Badiou's oeuvre. But in reality they are very different once one tries to realize them, since unilateral duality differs from the philosophical or transcendental triad. Marx's formula is, we might say, "ambiguous" like a unilateral duality, and gives a margin of play greater than Parmenides', owing to the fact that in not mentioning Thinking or *perceptio* (as Heidegger says), it does not evoke the third term of empirical reality as constitutive of the unilateral structure. Marx's formula can be read *as two or as three terms, depending on the perspective one takes upon it, depending on whether it is interpreted according to the fusion itself as radical immanence, or according to that supposed reality of the world, of philosophy and the masses in philosophy.* It is thus susceptible to a twofold interpretation: on one hand a philosophical ("ideological") or sufficient interpretation (one that destroys the originality of NP); and on the other an interpretation according to that immanence or Last Instance that endows philosophy with another status, no longer constitutive but occasional. Parmenides' formula is always read as having three terms—this is philosophy, which also dreams of this fusion but does not give itself the means or the right formula, giving it instead in the form of a pedagogy and a history wherein intellectuals find their role of mediation between the Masses and Theory, and philosophers end up as intellectuals devoting themselves also to the history and the explication of their "ideas." On the contrary, Marx's formula can be read as a possible generic formula that reduces mediation, without suppressing it pure and simple in favor of an immediate knowing. This is what NP calls the mediate-without-mediation or the *mediatum*: the participation of philosophical transcendence in radical immanence (with which, however, it is not to be conflated).

We can now explain why media intellectuals represent what we have called, for certain reasons, the "underclass" [*quart-monde*] of thought, that is to say the fourth [*quatrième*] world, which remains a world, but a deficient one. NP—of which they are the complete inversion, or the macroscopic or common sense—is organized according to a genetic element, radical immanence, which is also a quarter [*quart*]—but the quarter (-turn or -circle) becomes autonomous as imaginary or complex number (square root of -1), that is to say as vector, rather than the quarter-world [*quart-monde*], which still forms a world or aspires to be bathed in immanental appearance. And the quarter-world is like the inverted image of the quarter (-of-world). There is some kind of unintelligible attraction, a sort of fascination (but a unilateral one) between non-philosophy and this fourth figure that is, far more than its opposite, its abyssal image. The notion of a quarter-world only makes sense for a non-philosopher who, far from all Platonico-philosophical synthesis, avoids this antinomy via the quarter-turn as genetic element of theory and its fusion with subjects. One must therefore go right back to the "imaginary" root, to the quantware or the "logic" of the generic matrix, to perceive a procession other than that of Plato, one that Badiou attempts (in the "Second Manifesto"): a procession of truth or of the Idea in bodies. For it is a question of a recession of non-philosophy within philosophy. This is why intellectuals recount imaginary and specular conflicts without making works of philo-fiction; and why we can no longer define the task of thinking in terms of the struggle against the media alone. In the media or out of it, philosophy remains what it is.

How does Badiou situate himself in relation to this problematic? The planifier of hierarchies cannot allow himself this type of evaluation, this non-planification, he who seems to wish to and need to appropriate the intellectual descender (but who is threatened by it because of his ideal of purity), so as to conjugate it (as does every philosopher at this point) with the ascender of the Idea. In a certain way, he combines the two directive formulae, the long of Parmenides (who remains dominant) and the short of Marx (which in a certain way he destroys, as has been suggested, by combining it with Parmenides')—*a contradiction that is resolved by the topological operator of torsion as both ascender and descender*. His thought is a bow strung between two poles functioning together, philosophically: the Idea of Philosophy whose status he defends with his "manifestos," and, at the other end, the Idea of Communism. They are indissociable, and both refer from afar to mathematics as Platonic and materialist ideal of truth. This alliance for a common combat is explained in Badiou by reasons of taste and personal practice, rather than historical conjuncture. It is effectuated in traditional manner, but it must be admitted that this fusion of Communism and Truth, of People and Philosophy, relaying the Marxist fusion of masses and theory, is highly inspired, reinvigorating and far from mediocre—with purity, one has the advantage of being precise, at last, about what one is demanding... For our part, we call "gnostic" this great "revolutionary" ideal that buys into "strong thought" as a residual symptom of philosophical sufficiency, even if in its positing and in its realization this ideal remains abstract. Perhaps there is some sense here in bringing together Gnosticism and the generic against the *all*-philosophical, which Badiou also combats as *all*, to the point of making it difficult to know whether or not he develops a philosophy, whether it is not instead a great philosophy-without-philosophy. He has no "philosophy" except in the most banal sense—he is above all possessed *by* philosophy. Since Kant and Fichte, excluding and through Hegel, Nietzsche and Deleuze, "philosophers" are not so much "detached" theorists or thinkers of philosophy as *believers*, who naively invest their faith in their object. From this point of view, Badiou gives himself in philosophy a partial and very limited object, which is encompassing only in its formalism; but he puts all his faith in it. We shall turn against him his formula of philosophy as "disaster": Through an excess of means (not reduced, and delivered over to a general philosophical finality), he courts "intellectual disaster."

Non-philosophy as quarter-of-philosophy

Badiou begins by slicing into the philosophical tradition as into a particle or a closed world, between Plato and Aristotle—two halves of philosophy supposedly in either case complete. This is a traditional division that defines the philosopher, and which Badiou assumes, eliminating, for his part, Aristotle and beings (which are recuperated later, but always under condition of mathematics). He will in turn come under the objection of logicism, against a too-mathematical Plato—it is always the old problem of mathematics and/or biology, a duality that more or less short-circuits physics and that consequently appears to us neither pertinent nor effective. NP proceeds otherwise: certainly it also cuts into the all of philosophy—not as a closed world, but as symptom, and according to another type of non-philosophical or non-thematic cutting—without passing once again into the domains of being and of objects. This partitioning follows firstly the geometrical and physical (and thus scientific) model of quantum theory that it borrows, by half-circle and then by quarter-circle, so as to arrive at the minimal syntax that is vectorial. It must be thus always and in every way that NP has traversed *at least in appearance* the entire circle of the real. But what does it mean to say that philosophy has traversed its own circle? Badiou precisely gives himself philosophy as a closed corpuscle grasped from outside, which he cuts according to the philosophical hierarchy and its three orders (One, Being, beings), with each time a principal instance (even if three instances are convoked and two of them marginalized in favor of the remaining term). NP does not consider philosophy as such a corpuscle internal or external to itself; it begins by freeing itself from this amphiboly, treating it as an unlocalisable particle or an already-quantum symptom. This is what there is of the real in "Philosophy," its full circle being but an appearance that fools the philosopher, who installs himself there in good faith. NP therefore does not allow itself to be guided by the intra-philosophical hierarchy that inhabits this supposedly closed world. If one leaves philosophy to itself, it demands that one make a choice from this hierarchy—and, as absolute as this choice may be, it always presents itself as philosophically limited, as limited in scope, as is the case in Badiou. The philosopher is a philosopher of Being, of the One, and of beings in any case—each cultivates his own doublet, the third instance being marginalized. Badiou, like others, and despite his trenchant style, ceaselessly makes and remakes the full circle of philosophy, but does so in following this circle from the outside or from its margins, or else from inside its material contents or strata. Only a quantum theorist, and not a philosopher of philosophy, can take as a whole and without hierarchy, without totalization, the three instances whose totality is an appearance. Here again, the principle of non-commutativity is decisive: philosophy can no longer be its means and its end simultaneously, give or take a detail; that which in philosophy is a means cannot be convertible with that which, in it, can be submitted to an end. The famous initial line of demarcation that Deleuze identified so acutely, and with which all philosophers begin, is an intra-philosophical artifact destined to maintain philosophy in its rights and its claims. It constitutes itself at once proprietor and victim of the illusions of the proprietor, by positing an external or internal limit, saying "this is mine, this is my domain and the field over which I legislate." Philosophy is not "first" for nothing; it is that which declares itself first and possessor, forgetting the Prior-to-first of the underdetermining Condition.

5

Subtraction and superposition

From ontological difference to the superposition of the One

There can be no philosophy worthy of succeeding that of Heidegger and Deconstruction without a radical critique of ontological Difference, a critique of the thematic of difference in general in the name of a certain "identity," whether this difference be finite (Heidegger) or infinite (Deleuze). Here and there in contemporary philosophy, the problem is posed of the dissolution of philosophy's amphibolies or mixtures, whose typical form is given by "ontological Difference," whereas other philosophers (Deleuze, Derrida) claim to work within these mixtures, contenting themselves with loosening and retying otherwise the knots of thought. In all cases of dissolution, the recourse to an identity that is to be redefined is obviously fundamental. A new experience of identity and of the multiple is a means of invalidating the play of Difference from the outset, without having to meditate interminably on it as Heidegger does. But there are many heterogeneous experiences of identity, depending upon the ontological level at which one operates. It can be approached as the One-in-One according ultimately to itself, but the "in-the-last-instance," so as to avoid a vicious circle—it is in this way that NP mobilizes superposition rather than identification. Or else it can be approached according to and under the conditions of Being, which is what OV does. OV supposes a dialectical identity flattened onto itself, and which receives an immediate real status. NP "begins" by thinking identity itself, letting this identity be given as superposed and subtracted from its logical form through axioms. Thus it gives a real signification to the axiomatic, which itself unfolds from this test of identity. Immediate set-theoretical ontology—just like the ontology of life and of affectivity (Henry)—uses it only on condition of Being-without-beings. Only NP begins with the One-in-One or the One-without-Being and *a fortiori* without-beings, as undulatory superposition. Which does not at all exclude (on the contrary) a recourse to the contingency of transcendence (of philosophy, of sciences, of language, etc.) It can then give a status, albeit in-the-last-instance, to this purely phenomenal Same of idempotence in the manifold, for instance, of Being and beings, without supposing the constitutive role of one or the other reflected in itself and conditioning it.

Every other solution (even Henry's) comes back to conserving the amphibological form, albeit reduced to an immediate identity, as universal element or essence of thought. In these conditions which exclude the One-in-One, Being is not really subtracted from beings, if it is merely "subtracted" or "subtractive," but only from certain of their transcendent forms (perception, presence), so that it remains ordered by them. Only the One via superposition can subtract Being from beings themselves, just because it does not simply deny the latter as one once denied certain forms of beings, but consigns them to being secondary functions of the specification of Being (particulate materiality). In the same way, the transcendental ego (Henry) cannot really subtract Being from beings, because it still belongs to an auto-subtraction, and because the amphibological form, rather than being totally excluded from identity, subsists in it as repressed essence, or continues to co-determine the real. In Badiou, just as in Henry, thought is always exercised in the amphibological form as primary (this could even be said to be the philosophical and non-scientific "chamber" of these ways of thinking), even when it is a matter of identity—because the latter has not been, from the outset, of itself, acquired-as-given independently of that amphiboly-form that owes everything to logical identity. These attempts inevitably refer back surreptitiously to philo-sophical errors that they have never abandoned; not, doubtless, to a frank autoposition or difference, but to an autoposition that is merely truncated or inhibited. Insofar as identity will not be the object of a simple axiomatic (and real) "positing" *but one understood as superposition* (rather than the object of a philo-sophical auto-position that one confines oneself to initiating or limiting), it will not be able to free the amphiboly as such, or ontological Difference, and to treat it in positive manner, in terms of a relative autonomy of matter, but will find itself obliged to deny it, and to submit all the more to its incessant "returns."

Can one nevertheless, without doing anything more (that is to say without the return of the repressed) evacuate ontological Difference through means that themselves remain ontological? On its Platonic side, ontology is constructed around the One and the Multiple—it is a transcendental arithmetic, Pythagorean in origin. On its Aristotelian side, it is constructed rather around Being and beings—it is an onto-theology. But philosophy, in its real breadth and its concreteness, is the intrication of these two dyads. It is the quadripartite that tolerates a certain convertibility that was present from the origins of the One and of Being, and which has been overdetermined and interpreted according to these two contexts. If, by modernity, one understands the isolation of the One-Multiple from the other correlation, this is done with the aim of withdrawing from it all trace of the latter, understood as "presence," and devoting it to an objectivism which, measured according to concrete ontological Difference, amounts to a sort of flattening of the latter, to an immediate identity of Being and beings in the avowed favour of Being. But the thematic of Difference is then merely repressed, and risks returning from its mathematico-modern repression. *Being and Event* supposes a certain affect of Being as Being "in-itself," grasped outside all subjective immanence, as absolute, quasi-thing-oriented, substantial and inert (albeit multiple) objectivity. This is an immediate identity of the object and objectivation:

Being thus appears to have abolished beings, but it is also just as much beings that triumph over Being. Such is the ambiguity of an ontology that postulates the merely philosophical destruction of ontological Difference as difference: it does not say what it is, and it is not what it says; it calls itself an ontology, but is realized as an ontical experience and thought, or even as a determinate knowledge produced by the sciences.

How, moreover—through what experience, what knowledge—is this affect of the "in-itself" realized? Arithmetic immediately receives a usage that is ontological and (let us say it clearly) supposedly real. The One itself cannot be deposed and ejected from Being, to become once more the one of calculation, without also being the equivalent of the one of language, of closure, of the limit, of transcendent determination, of the unity of a predicate, of a quality, of a property, of the unit of an operation, etc. Again, it is a question, despite everything, of a transcendental count, but a truncated one. In general, OV "slims down" Pythagorean and Platonic mixtures of arithmetic and metaphysics, reducing their metaphysical side, whereas for Being as transcendental entity, it substitutes the void and the infinite. All the same, these mixtures remain abstract modes, through the partition implied by the "ontology of Presence"— that is to say the Difference between Presence and the Present, between Being and beings. Here they are simply "flattened," without distance or difference, into an immediate identity—the "materialist dialectic." In this way, set-theoretical arithmetic remains held fast immediately in a transcendental usage, and receives a real or ontological signification.

We admit all the same that to demonstrate that Badiou utilizes the classical schema of philosophy, more hermeneutic than axiomatic, is by no means a simple task. We may sometimes give the impression of subjecting him to an unfair trial. His axiomatic style allows the positing of affirmations or theses with a tranquil assurance and a self-evidence, with apodictic and finite effects that can only intimidate and leave the reader with no recourse. Even philosophy, which is only possible, without being expected, arrives in parousia, as if it fell to us from the stars, when it is already too late and the chips are down. We must identify the subtle dissimulations that allow him to leap from plane to plane and to go back down naturally to the most materialist planes of philosophy—the mechanism of topological torsion in particular. Doubtless one of the causes of his enterprise is that modern arithmetic ceases to be reflected by a preconstituted ontology and, in Cantor, "reflects" on itself; so that this metaphysics now exceeds set-theoretical immanence and can safely be evacuated as obsolete. But Cantorian mathematical "auto-reflection" takes over from Difference; a mixture in the form of presence is replaced by another mixture in the form of immediate (albeit unilateral) identity. Beings themselves are not completely suspended—only their effectuation as transcendent One-Multiple is suspended, as quasi-perceptual and ontical Unity and Particularity. The particularity of beings has indeed been abolished, but only their "Aristotelian" particularity; it has been replaced by that which is procured no longer by perception but by a knowledge (here, mathematical knowledge), and through the particular specialism of that knowledge, the Multiple. Ontological Difference, evidently, was but the idealization and interiorization of the model of perception. It suffices to resort to mathematics, to the identity of the concept and the mathematical object, to posit that of Being and of beings, and to believe thereby to have really surpassed ontological Difference. In fact, here there is only an empirical surpassing of Difference, not at all its real critique. The substitution of immediate mathematical auto-reflection for perceptual auto-reflection is an intra-ontic transformation whose effect is to dissimulate ontological Difference rather than to really invalidate it. The subtraction of arithmetic from perception, of Being-beings from ontological Difference, supposes an immediate identity of "contraries"—a sort of condensation or crystallization of ontological Difference, but not at all its suppression, as we are asked to believe. Truncated, inhibited Difference; a Difference whose absence is compensated for by this immediate autoposition, under the auspices of Cantorian "reflection," of which mathematics is capable, and which is now the autoposition of the void.

Taking the problem from another angle, Being is not only nothingness, non-being; it is, so it seems, the void. And yet this void, devoid of all transcendent determination, despite everything remains a nothingness: determined not by any particular being but by *beings*. For Being is here the ultimate or foundational point of view of philosophy; and if there is an identity in question here, it is a surreptitious and denied one, an ineffective identity. How to obtain a Being really void of all beings and even of any ultimate and secret reference to beings? For this we need the One: Being is thus (not-) One, and it is on this condition that it is really void of beings, and not merely nothingness. The One-in-the-last-instance, the absolutely non-mixed, radicalizes the void of Being, delivers it from the ultimate ontical-formal closure (without for all that negating or denying the latter). It is radical immanence, or immanence through superposition.

Radical immanence via idempotent addition

Materialist immanence belongs to procedures of division and position, and consequently to the double transcendence that forms the essence of philosophy. Let us therefore take a detour via the various manners in which radical immanence is philosophically said or formulated, taking them in and transforming them into undulatory or superposable form, obtained by idempotent addition and no longer by division. They will be as follows: (1) A metaphysical contribution: statements on the One or the Indivisible (Plato) or the All (Levinas), but "axiomatised" generically, or deprived of their philosophical sense, of their doublet-form or of duplicity. Radical immanence is then that which is "resumed" rather than that which "repeats"— this operation exists but is immediately effaced. It does not double itself across a division, but resumes itself. It is a radical Undivided that therefore can never be an All, a Same if you like; that will never return on itself and will not be adjoined synthetically to itself to make a Two and thereby an All. No point in trying to imagine it—you will not find it—it is the

Real-in-person; (2) A phenomenological contribution, equally metaphysical: the Same as object or thing, the transcendent identity of a multiplicity of adumbrations (the metaphysical principle of Aristotle, Leibniz, Frege, Husserl, Quine, etc.: geometrical invariants, imaginary variations, or eidetic essences as invariants), but an identity or invariant from here on deprived of its multiplicity, of the transcendent form of this identity. More subtly, identity here risks losing the possibility of repetition that it must have, if it has no multiple; but one can suppose that philosophy has in general protected itself against this problem present in Parmenides and in atomism, or again in the Platonic Idea, separated and lifeless, quasi-atomic (before the *Sophist*), or before the deconstruction of ideality that brings out its repetitious nature. Here again, we can posit as the before-first term a Same in which co-exist the resumption and the particulate effacement of the corpuscular Two of repetition—what NP calls the resumption of immanence, to distinguish it from the usual repetition; (3) A religious contribution—gnostic, in fact: *gnosis* or the knowledge that we are without knowing it. This is to claim to know reflexively or through a doubled transcendence this first knowledge that perturbs and destroys it, unless one finds that this knowledge is already virtually one of superposition, and is thus the object of a knowledge via super-position that does not perturb it, leaves it constant, but on the other hand changes its usage by transforming it into a variable or a means. This generic knowing is without direct object or reference, since it is immanence. Such a generic gnosis is now deprived of its religious (still transcendent) sense (an atheist

gnosis), and we must find for it another, non-religious "content";
we must transform gnosis in parallel with metaphysics and
phenomenology; (4) Fichte's I = I, the cause of both truth and
transcendental illusion, but to be interpreted as a superposition
of I with itself and with the non-I.

Hermeneutic of quantum axioms (oraxioms)

What happens in the generic matrix? NP appeals to the
formalism of algebra, to the property of idempotence, in order
to understand the principle of superposition. It is thus not a
mere means of calculation, it is also to be read in the matrix
according to a "silent," non-thematic philosophy. This sort
of silent "meta-philosophy" (in reality, a non-philosophy) of
science is registered and justified in the matrix through the
existence of an inclusive or generic lived, itself extracted from
the philosophical subject, so that the autonomy of philosophy
will be but an appearance—contrary to the meta-ontological
point of view on mathematics. In the latter, the necessity of
philosophy's intervention is resolved in a Moebian manner,
whereas in NP it is distributed *in a silent or lived usage as
wave function, and in a unifacial linguistic particle (or noematic
subject) that can be apparently or objectively given also, as
in-itself.* Unlike the quantum theory of matter, which supposes
a macroscopic world in-itself and runs up against antinomies or
exclusions once it broaches the microscopic (antinomies that it

resolves through mathematical deduction), the quantum theory of philosophy supposes that the world in-itself of philosophy is posited as symptom or objective appearance.

For one must necessarily give oneself philosophy as a symptom that can always become an in-itself fabricated in appearance. If one gives it to oneself naively, as a true in-itself, by practicing philosophy spontaneously, then it becomes impossible to escape this appearance, which is then taken not only objectively, but as the sole absolute reality. The point of view of the quantum stance or of lived immanence that gives access to philosophy as simply objective appearance is capable of falling under science, which is what we have elsewhere called the immanent identity *of or for* philosophy. Naive philosophy is the absolute, but the radical that is valid only for lived immanence makes of the absolute a well-founded appearance.

The other consequence is that NP's axiomatic includes a moment of invention or interpretation no longer at the formal algebraic level of axioms, but in their incarnated or linguistic, hylomorphic or "unilational" part, that part favorable to a hermeneutics. Axiomatisation-interpretation is also partitioned by a unilateral complementarity that reproduces the duality of the lived wave function and the particular form-subject that is unilateral, and succeeds in constituting the generic constant. The unilational axiom is now understood as immanent wave function or as amplitude, and moreover as conceptual particle, oriented as unilateral and unifacial. This helps us better grasp the duality of the unilational axiom: axioms in general are linguistic, or refer to the reality of language or of logic, but not to the radical Real; they are multiple and empty although they must be under-determined or immanent and radical. *We shall call oraxiom the superposition of axiomatic decision and philosophical decision, the quantum superposition that transforms concepts and their effects.* This structure of NP necessitates its being practiced in such a way that one invents NP itself with the aid of its object, since it is from this object (an interfering object) that is extracted the lived-without-subject that is pre-empted by the purely scientific apparatus. We do not read the text of an axiomatic science formulated already elsewhere, and laid out upon the empty mirror of Being. This sage and conservative meta-ontology as an image is not at all appropriate to the necessity of inventing, on a minimal basis, axioms incarnated according to their object. There is a hermeneutic aspect of the apparatus that is susceptible, as subject-noema, to formulations also drawn from the object. This is an entirely different science in itself, but one whose axiomatic apparatus is capable of multiple formulations or fictional and superposed enunciations, depending on the object. Algebraic formalism finds its unilateral complement in a quasi-hermeneutics in the form of a "probabilist" fiction. This interpretation of axioms means that philosophy is not merely a material, but a sort of model for NP. Reciprocally, philo-fiction has a determinate hermeneutic aspect, but one that is determinate in-the-last-instance or under-determined by quantum theory.

If NP, from the outset, introduces the subject in scientific conditions, and thus resolves the problem of the agent-operator or that of the no longer external observer, then the interpretation (but also the possibility in principle) of macroscopic reduction/destruction are integrated a priori into the apparatus. There is a fusion in-the-last-instance ("unified theory") of science and of philosophy, but under the conditions of science, not those of philosophy. This is the Marxist schema of the fusion of theory and the masses that makes possible a proletarian science, but without the external proletarian predicate. It imposes the unity of axioms and of their interpretation according to the philo-sophical symptoms, but under the conditions of the axiomatic.

There is thus no need to distinguish transcendently the axiomatic from meta-ontology; their unity is effectuated in the axiomatic, but such that algebra (which is not a science of the object) is no longer detained here in a transparent head-to-head with its meta-ontological interpretation. Axioms are no longer read in meta-ontological or topological distance, but posited as a priori fusion of the axiomatic matrix (unilateral duality as function of the lived) and of their interpretation—the unity of science and of the subject, in global terms. Meta-ontology and the logical transcendental are only stitched-together philosophical juxtapositions of given sciences, mathematics and the logic of categories—they are the work of a reading and a rearrangement of sciences, of their external combination in philosophical space, and not that of the invention of a generic science.

The science-subject as generically unified theory (GUT)

Can one suppose, under these new generic conditions, that every science (even the most positive and objective) can be transformed to contain a subject of science, like psychoanalysis—or better still, would be a mode of a science that is the generic science *par excellence*, that of humans, and would be in reality a *science-subject conveying a subjective but generic determination that belongs to its object*? In this case, the sciences would be neither regional nor universal in the philosophical mode, but instead generic— something that would permit them to rejoin art, love and politics, which have a more obvious relation to the lived included in their procedures, but which, for their part, must acquire a dimension of objective knowledge. This would be a more radical understanding of the "subject of science"—neither science of the subject nor the philosophical subject of science, but a science-subject that would permit us to put all knowledge under condition of the human in the Last Instance. Even those positive sciences that seem to know nothing of the subject or of the lived would "symptomatize" on the basis of the science of humans as immanent model of all science. This hypothesis is appropriate, moreover, to an ethics that makes of man not the last end, but the last line of defense that must bring together all the disciplines that are human only in ultimate manner (this last caveat saving also the positivity of the sciences).

This solution of a generically unified theory amounts to treating knowledges as means one in relation to the other. We make them into variables whose inverse multiplications are inequalities. To treat them as variables is to make of them reciprocal means of generic "translation" with re-quantification or resumption. We establish *a principle of non-commutativity of means, insofar as they are not any means whatsoever* but are philosophical and scientific in origin. The principle of the non-commutativity of means destroys them in their broad philosophical specularity, and is the ultimate way to deliver them to the generic or to make a generic usage of them. We oppose this theoretical ethics to Badiou, who slices and cuts (but not longitudinally) strata that are still disciplinary, tracing the traditional philosophical edifice according to the hierarchy of great instances, rather than taking it as the concrete totality of a new object within which a human science must impose its own system of partition. The philosopher can be recognized through his accepting philosophy such as it presents itself, as already reflected in itself. This, of course, becomes a repetitive exercise that turns endlessly in its own space; but there are laws of this circular space of philosophy which should be sought out, and which involve accepting the circle as circular, but seeing it also as the object of a unilateral or fractured science. Philosophy as tradition is this game of musical chairs between great instances, a combinatorial that is still rather impoverished, like musical "tonality," and which must be unfettered. NP's initial project was to *serialize the standard tonality of the philosophical scale*—to treat all of its pitches equally, as parameters or variables, so as to make heard a music other than the classical—this initiative proceeding from a personal imaginary that is, no doubt, more musical than pictorial (unlike that of the French phenomenologists).

Recalling of the global generic effect

NP as generic science, supposing a certain usage of the principles of quantum theory, cannot be confused with procedures drawn from philosophy and simply varied or differenced. Certainly, its procedures are complicated and may lead to a true, ultimately mathematical, formalism. But if the complexity of its objects provide the means for this, the generic effect is another thing altogether. Recall that it is produced by two principles foreign to philosophy: superposition understood as resumption of radical immanence, and non-commutativity understood as determination-in-the-last-instance. NP is only the placing-under-condition (to which Badiou limits himself), but an under-determining one, of the opinion or of the representation organized by philosophy. These two principles express what it calls the Real, which is not especially Being nor the One nor the Multiple (these are metaphysical contents). The affinity of science and the One-in-One is made explicit by these two principles. It provides at once the Real and syntax, immanence and order as prior-to-priority or non-commutativity.

It is necessary to reconsider the theme of Cartesian doubt, Fichtean doubt, and above all the phenomenological neutralization that Husserl qua mathematician thought to be the science-effect. Husserl gave it a transcendental and thus subjective form, dominant and determinative of the real—a little like Kant, but more ambiguous, in truth. We must reverse Husserl's position: it is immanental science-as-subject that determines the object as a function of the Real. This reversal signifies the passage from a transcendental idealism (which opposes essentially mathematical objective ideality to psychological subjectivity) to a generic science (which opposes indirect and quantum objectivity to direct mathematical objectivity).

Whence the suspension of analysis and synthesis—operations more philosophical than scientific, even if their bedrock is found in logico-mathematical properties. Already the transcendental was understood as that which determines, through and as ideality, the empirical object. NP opposes to ideality not an empirical and still philosophical real, but the immanental Real that is determined by two principles capable of generating an indirect objectivity. It is not a transcendental, but an immanental quantum-theoreticism, that, in this sense, neutralizes ideality itself—that is to say, the Platonism of the true Idea—by reducing it to a simple or particulate transcendence.

Real, logic, and algebra: Kant's objection

Kant's objection as to the use of general logic, which creates transcendental appearances, does not make a great deal of sense against the introduction of algebra in NP. On the one hand, it is impossible to avoid the encounter of logic and/or mathematics with the real; this is a general constraint that, in a sense, is imposed by any philosophical-type thought that cannot be reduced to a simple conceptual reflection. On the other hand, the non-philosophical context is neither transcendental-synthetic nor logico-analytic, which excludes transcendental illusion. It is tighter or narrower, algebraic and immanental, at once analytic and synthetic in a new proportion (unilateral duality) which excludes the transcendental without denying its virtues.

The most general form of the governing equation is *algebraic idempotence = real or radical immanence*. It is comparable, from afar, to *mathematics = ontology*, lived idempotence playing a role similar to that of the empty set, and precisely founding unilaterality as what we call in *Non-Standard Philosophy* the analytic-strong and the synthetic-weak. This equation supposes the reduction of logic to the idempotent connective alone (just as, respectively, mathematics is reduced to set-theory); and the reduction of the real to immanence alone (just as the real is reduced to being, and being to the inconsistent multiple). Because with simply analytic identity, immanence would remain like a critical margin of philosophy—we see this in Kant, who constructs the synthetic in the borders of the analytic (inaugu-rating thereby all of contemporary marginalism); and according to Fichte (logic understood as identity of I = I), real immanence would then be simply avowed to transcendental illusion. We may wonder whether the identification of mathematics and ontology, cut off from philosophy (which thereby conserves something of the function that metaphysics plays in Kant), does not repeat the confusion of general logic with the philosophical real, in favor this time of a materialist metaphysics (many things having changed in the meantime, mathematics replacing logic with another status). But in the case under consideration, the style of identification remains globally under the authority of a philosophical decision, even though mathematics claims an autonomy apparently inaccessible to logic. As for NP, it also (even more so) could give rise, with its own equation, to the same objection of the Kantian transcendental dialectic to the confusion of general logic with the real. Everything depends then on the degree or the type of autonomy of logic or of mathematics, the type of "hole" that they make in philosophy (presence, representation, the logos) supposed as given. We must compare the power of the empty set with that of idempotence with regard to Being: the power of the Void that subtracts, with the Last Instance that virtualizes.

All the same, if a "decision" is impossible in the supposed context of a transcendental dialectic, since the two positions are equivalent in being prey to this confusion, such a decision would become possible were philosophy not unwarrantedly supposed given as in the first case, but as in principle given precisely *with and by* the real instance of idempotence that makes the "hole" in its identity or, in any case, in its authority. For non-philosophy, far from proceeding under the initial and final authority of philosophy, supposing it given without proof and defending it all the more violently, frees itself from philosophy as authority, but not as material or occasion, in the sense that it gives itself philosophy under the condition of science insofar as it has an access in principle to it, an access that is not questioned in the materialist equation. *The major, general problem with philosophical decisions—their arbitrariness—stems from giving oneself access in principle to philosophy in the form of a contingent, factual access, or a traditional access that has not been problematized.*

The real of NP is not that which transcendental dialectic targets—a transcendent and metaphysical real destined to give rise to antitheses (Kant). Nor, beyond mathematics, the being that would be the object of logic (Badiou). Instead, it is an immanental logic that, through a pre-empting of the lived, "draws the conclusion" of the real from the property of idempotence. Immanental logic—this is what NP is in its "foundation" in-the-last-instance. Idempotence is a property become, through its lived tenor, an operator that has as its real, at least, its proper neutralized form and the lived. Its tenor is not an oriental-type absolute void, neither is it a set-theoretical void, an inconsistent multiple. Materialist ontology goes from the inconsistent multiple to the void, that of idempotence goes from the operatory manifold to the Same of *Idem-*; but both, and perhaps above all the latter, avoid the arithmetical positivism of set theory. We must follow to their ultimate effects *the empty set* and *algebraic idempotence*. They operate at the same functional level, but idempotence is not the void, and refuses to install thought in the void of truth, installing it instead in the neutrality or sterility of a Logos become silent and clandestine—the Stranger. Where the philosopher reads, in mathematics, an ontology of the void and of the subtractive act in relation to the world, the non-philosopher reads in this algebraic property a sub-ontology, an onto(-logy) (simplified or without doublet) of addition or of superposition, but not of the full—*an ontology of the neutralization and sterilization of philosophical surplus-value.* An "ontology" of sterilization or of non-capitalist transformation, rather than one of subtractive and anti-capitalist truth.

The problem is that of the ultimate referent or the measure of the real. Is the transcendental zero as mathematical being, void of world? Or is it the minimal of world, the *minimum of world* necessary for the algebra that can neutralize or sterilize it? We must choose between the void of the world (in truth, precisely a dialectical appearance) and the minimum of world, between the void and evil as the residue of transcendence left by the generic neutralization. This minimum of evil-world is not denied, in materialist manner, in the name of the mathematical void, but maintained in reality in the form of philosophy and in the form of an integrism of philosophy that ceaselessly returns like a repressed evil. It is, in this case, the minimum X of transcendence that resists immanence itself, because it is attached to the transcendental despite its passage or its fall into immanence. A remainder of transcendence is attached to immanence, just as the set-form is attached to zero or to the void. The whole difference between the two theories, NP and OV, resides in the qualitative dosage of transcendence and immanence. There is always this mélange if one measures them reciprocally—but less so (perhaps not at all) in the first, which reasons in terms of minimal evil, than in the second, which denies pure and simple its principal existence, evil being understood not ontologically but ontically, as a degradation of void philosophy into beings. NP installs itself in the world without re-cognizing itself in it, and for this reason can transform it—it makes an ethical practice possible. Whereas OV is Platonic, acosmic, and thinks the subject as eternal and immortal, at the risk, through an excess of theoreticism, of not understanding the degradation or the fall that it fears. It has no ethics, apart from an ethics as magical practice of the Verb and as political augury.

We oppose the immanental generic lived to quasi-transcendental mathematicism, symbols without ontic content but with a lived content to objects in the void of set theory. If one takes as one's endpoint philosophy as transcendental, then algebra is the last possible point of retreat, the starting point—*not as identity and contradiction, but instead as idempotence and super-position*. But if one takes philosophy reduced to materialism as a measure, the true limit of possible retreat is mathematics, if not logic. The whole problem is therefore that of knowing whether logic itself is measured by the principle of identity or by idempotence. The latter is analytic, with a synthetic tendency or disposition—two non-mixed aspects, both of which are mixed in any case in philosophy, which is at once analytic and synthetic.

Finally, a last objection against NP: is not the idea of the (logical) connective contemporary with beings (or with the Ones that it connects or binds), whereas the inconsistent multiple of mathematics and the zero of the empty set would be contem-porary with Being rather than with the One? But the set-form remains a transcendental form, like Being itself, and is ultimately contaminated by that of Being—a transcendence whose double form is our principal adversary; whereas the idempotence-form remains ontologico-scientific and not ontologico-philosophical, since it does not reenter the frameworks of a classical ontology. The idempotence-form manipulates the One, but not the One of metaphysics nor the arithmetical One or the unit-of-count, not beings. Idempotence is not itself the One as added or as multiplied unit-of-count; it is a Same: One + One = One. There would be surplus-value or a different result only if the One of idempotence, the Same, were reduced to the ideal identity of the beings-ones that are but its terms or givens, and cannot be conflated with the Idempotent, which is neither beings nor Being.

Subtraction and the problem of schematism

The problem is that of the thinking of the Real qua subtracted from the concept and from the law, not only from sophism and from certain forms of representation; as subtracted from the authorities that are collected by Badiou under the term of the One. It is thus the disjunction One/Multiple that governs subtraction on different levels. Badiou chooses to take as reference not the rock of representation, but specific theorems or axioms that come to be lodged in the "difference" One/Multiple or One/Void. It is not a difference that would be a mixture; it is the *philosophically* materialist immanence that detaches itself from the One or subtracts itself from the One of presence, supporting itself upon axioms or theorems.

Mathematics itself does not determine philosophy, but simply, like the infinite, subtracts it from its concept. Meta-ontological decision is the custodian of subtraction from the concept, knowledge or count, from the poem, from amorous fusion; that which operates its auto-subtraction with the aid of mathematics or another generic procedure. This is to suppose that philosophy is valid as authority and as giver of ultimate sense, as the measure of subtraction. It is to conceive the generic in the wide sense as an alterity in relation to the law of evaluation, the mark of difference, the finite, and ultimately in relation to the proper name or to nomination—a way of classifying the types of alterity according to that from which they are subtracted, specifying the lack, the default, the void. Thus, no kind of new materiality is gained by this operation. Finally, the type of alterity or of real in relation to that from which it is subtracted, is not a difference: the void or the infinite is an exteriority without difference—here is the real novelty, but what novelty? These subtractions are each time supported by mathematical theorems (the non-denumerable, the generic, etc.). Or else these theorems suffice to themselves, and the subtractive as empty category is a contemplative and Platonist guardian (above all if it is void and must remain so) of being qua being. Or else the theorems do not suffice, of themselves, to excavate the void, and they must themselves also be aided by a philosophical act. It seems that here, precisely, we find a strange relation, a non-relation, exercised mathematically by the positivity of a theorem, which in itself has no especial philosophical significance but which must be philosophically or categorially contemplated. Badiou wishes to avoid the Kantian schematism, which is, for him, obscure—for he does not know the transcendental, or the transcendental apperception with which he confuses it. His is a contemplative theoreticism. Perhaps with the transcendental One we have a function of schematization, but this latter is the problem of the acute duality concept/space, and thus is a function of the transcendental imagination that fills the One, at least on the plane of effectivity. Badiou eliminates the transcendental One and schematization—he returns to Plato. So what does he place between the empty category of subtractive truth and the mathematics that they require? A pre-established harmony, a harmony once more between the philosophical categoriality that is legislative for mathematics and generic truths, and mathematics in its positive autonomy—which in itself has no idea or will to grasp itself as ontology or as thought of being qua being. It seems that the effective possibility of subtraction would be assured principally by mathematics, and then philosophically endowed with a void categorial meaning. The subtractive, or that form of alterity, seems a mystery, which is not so much *différe/ance*, since Derrida presupposes the symptom as mélange of identity and spontaneous alterity that is then aggravated, and that one thus gives to oneself rather than deciding. Badiou remains within philosophy, and exerts a new decision that is regressive in relation to Derrida: he suppresses from the outset the problem of mélanges and of contamination. The stellar aspirant having, for his part, rejected presence and the whole inferior part of Platonism as null and void, makes his ascent uniquely in the superior part of Platonism, from the mathematical plane established as sufficient toward the philosophical Good. We might wonder whether it is really possible to operate a genealogy of the disasters of philosophy that he rejects, without according them, for example, the same relative sufficiency as do Heidegger and Derrida (who at least take the trouble of carrying out a certain genealogy without simply reducing them to that catch-all procedure of the "confusion" of planes). This is the problem of the "Kantian" schematism, and of what remains of it in all philosophers insofar as they ceaselessly live between earth and sky, seeking the optimal conciliation of the two.

The non-theological solution to the schematism: From transcendental imagination to imaginary number

We know that the schematism is essentially religious or at least that, qua "schematization," it supports a Christian interpretation. It is not surprising that it returns to haunt all systems of double transcendence. In its Kantian and Heideggerian form, the most well-known form, it is charged with regulating the old problem of the unity of contraries of the concept and the empirical; in Hegel, more broadly, that of the rational and the real; and in Badiou that of mathematics and being (the equation mathematics = ontology)—a problem for which he apparently finds a new, topological, solution. In NP, the problem of the combination of algebraic (quantum) givens and philosophical lived givens, their reciprocal interpretation, so to speak, is a neighbouring problem, and one that is liable to evoke it. But we seek another approach than that of the schematism (which supposes an hierarchical, empirico-rational, decidedly too simplistic dualism) and its solution via the transcendental imagination, which can only fall on one of two sides, thus only accentuating the hierarchy (the opposed solutions of Hermann Cohen and Heidegger), or its solution through topology, which also leaves subsisting the philosophical doublets as another hierarchical organization (planification). This other (quantum) solution does not posit an immediate identity of contraries. It consists in multiplying one by the other the two variables in question, in considering their products and, in a second stage, in adding them through superposition rather than through unification. Hegel is on the way to this with the dialectic of the understanding, but (apart from the fact that he proceeds via negation) he allows himself to be absorbed ultimately by the doubling of transcendence or by the rational. Now, NP's solution is essentially quantum-theoretical, scientific, rather than dialectical or philosophical. It supposes that the multiplication one by the other of the (algebraic and philosophical) variables is possible and necessary, because of a certain closure of the milieu of experience in which they are engaged, rather than their being left in the unlimited or ill-structured fuzziness of the philosophical space where everything is possible. The matrix is a chamber that is not totally closed or enclosed—we shall say "completed but not closed"—a matrix that prevents the variables from dispersing, along with their effects, and constrains them to be combined (compare the transcendental imagination, closed upon itself in a repeatable circle, and such an experimental chamber as collider, not closed upon itself). In short, we take account not only of variables as particles, but also take the space where they function as a quantum phenomenon or as state vectors. We must then take account of the products of contraries (here, quantum givens and philosophical givens) and be able to add them as symbols to obtain one state vector or wave function.

Now, why should this chamber not be closed, double-locked, absolutely closed? That would be a perfect circle. Half-closed, half-open, then? That would be a too quantitative and transcendent determination. Well then, not closed upon itself in the manner of a circle that repeats to the infinite, and thus prevented from closing or stopping mid-course? That would still be a positive version of quantum theory and of the undulatory. Stopped, rather, at the point of the subtraction of the first quarter of the circle; opened by its first quarter turn, but no more. It is the hole as quarter that makes the imaginary (in the sense of the imaginary or complex number) in the diverse, conceptual or intuitive arithmetical or representative closures. *It is the imaginary that opens or exceeds transcendental imagination itself as philosophical closure*, and which is specific to the state vector or to quantum phenomena. The quantum chamber is open a quarter-hole, no more—otherwise it would be once more measurable as a transcendent phenomenon and thus once more philosophizable. Auto-philosophical critiques, where science answers to philosophy, have no value. They remain of the order of the psycho-transcendental imaginary that is reflected in itself, and attains no heteronomy from the mathematical imaginary.

One last pass: this "quartial" (not exactly "partial") opening, which has no equivalent in philosophical transcendence, is essentially algebraic, not transcendental. It is, however, ambiguous—for it could be, as far as we know at this point, of the order of a physical and positive phenomenon. It must therefore itself be reduced and brought back down within the limits of radical immanence, of a chamber that alone can pare down or efface what remains of double transcendence in it. But this immanence must remain essentially a quantum immanence, operated by a science and thus as rigorous as possible. The solution consists in substituting quantum superposition for the unity of imagination. Finally, the chamber we evoked above could be called a generic apparatus for the production of knowledges, of the "collider" type. The schematism that is content to "regulate" a problem, to bring to it a solution even if a rather tautological one, is now surpassed by a production of knowledges that is assured by the passage from a limited concept to a rigorous concept of the imaginary or of philo-fiction. The philosophical givens are no longer alone in programming a "theological" solution; from now on, it will be invented with the aid of other knowledges.

The real non-act and its action through potentialization

OV and NP seem to begin in the same way—with a certain passivity linked now to materialism, now to real immanence. Through a non-decisional decision-(of)-self or a non-positional positing-(of)-self in the former, through a state of non-positional superposition-(of)-self in the latter. But we must distinguish the philosophical *decision* that is suspended or suspends itself, is simply delayed or put into waiting, from the *state* of superposition or resumption that affects philosophy from the outset.

Badiou qualifies his operation of thinking as subtraction and as subtractive, probably because it is for him a materialist way to possess philosophy provisionally to any initiative, particularly a transcendental or conditioning or possibilizing initiative. How, then, is subtraction "possible," if the problem can still be posed? The identity of the empty Set and Being, as unequal as it might be, is the absolute condition of set-theoretical ontology, and suffices to assure the subtractive aspect of the mathematical side. But this identification is a decision that then vanishes into itself or into its effect, an axiomatic decision, a condition that subtracts itself from conditioning, and that stands in a priority over mathematical practice. But what is it to Being? Why would Being accept to be subtracted from presence, why would it consent to this? It must be admitted that mathematics pre-empts it over the philosophical all, something that Badiou cannot admit—this is the operation that he does not seem to have prepared, on one side or the other. So it seems likely that the basis of materialist ontology remains suspended, as subtraction, at the eminently philosophical convenience of meta-ontological transcendence. The identification of the (empty) set and Being seems problematic because of the resistance of philosophy to its subtraction from presence.

As for NP, how does it (if it does indeed succeed in doing so) go to the end of the philosophical decision, a decision that does not even have any longer to consent to its subtraction or its mathematical annulation? Given that it claims explicitly a duality of the quantum theoretical and the philosophical decision, the affair seems to be off to a bad start. NP seems to affect with negation all the positive terms, the possible becoming the impossible, the visible becoming invisible, etc. Now, this is not a negation (either dialectical or immediate) of attributes taken from the world or from philosophy either by itself (cataphatic philosophy) or by the Real. For the Real via immanence cannot deny anything of the world; it is a non-acting that is foreclosed or indifferent to it, and which, from this point of view, entertains an affinity with materialism—but only an apparent one, for it is a lived materiality and not a materialist position. The "non" is therefore not an all-powerful negation. It has a status or function only at a level that is no longer dialectical, no longer at the level of signifier and sense, but that of usage; it is a "non" that affects the usage of terms, a lived that transforms them. But it is acquired not through a presupposed identification or a dialectical autoposition, but by superposition, which supposes the quantum theoretical and non-philosophico-corpuscular milieu. As the radical immanence of the Real is in its essence a non-acting, it must be that it makes itself an act or organon qua immanent, an a priori that is an action through neutralization of double transcendence, but certainly not a mechanical effect. Superposition subtracts simple particulate transcendence from its form-doublet, and it is a depotentialization; but evidently there is no "subtraction in itself," only *a subtracted-without-subtraction that is the superposed state of immanence, and, moreover, a subtraction as act that is originally corpuscular, and then particulate*. We shall oppose the (superpositional) state-([of]-self) to the decision of the thesis, but at the same time we shall recognize as necessary a certain intervention of the philosophical act qua symptom or resumption of non-acting. Rather than posit a dogmatic decision fallen from the stars, and then seem to deny it, it is precisely the duality of the initial decision of the fusion of the Set and Being that will permit us far more clearly to say what is being done, and to do what we say, in their distinction or in their unilateral duality—rather than to stun subjects with the violence of the decision of the void that is nothing less than void of decision. The *non-* is the One as *non-*(Being), but such that non-Being is one subtracted from the duplicitous Being of presence, a simplification of Being as doublet, and as become a generic a priori. Subjects must consent clearly to this act, implicating themselves in the situation and ceasing to contemplate it. Against the passive and flattening materialist position, subjects must consent actively to the materiality of their lived. These terms transformed by NP are not "immediate negations" (Henry). Even where originally positive, they become immediate liveds, or are unfolded. Not absence or lack, for example, to name the Real, but the "lived-(of)-absence" or the "lived-(of)-lack," which thus suppose, in order to be legitimated, a work that is in fact non-Lacanian.

The (of) in parentheses indicates an immediation or an immanence of the Real for that which pertains to its transcending as particle, that is to say the undulatory a priori of the Other-than... by which this immanence of the Real sets itself to transcending (ascending) and fulfills the role of an organon. Now, philosophy, which also counts on a moment of immediation, does so too fast, or only does so for an organon separated as an instrument, tool or mediation. Why? Because in philosophy immediation is doubled or duplicitous, whereas it must be mobilized only once, to manifest it as organon or a priori. The Logos therefore no longer constitutes a world in itself, but is transformed "from within," simplified or unfolded according to the dimension of immanence and its superposition, not according to a transversal or diagonal (which would obviously lead back to the space of the Moebius band). NP transforms the statements of the Logos by inserting them into a generic plane (*an immanence that transcends once each time*). It deploys and unfolds according to a generic plane the folded or duplicitous statements of philosophy. All this work is done on the level of the subject, completed with the subject. It is a work of the production of first names or of an unfolding on the generic plane (the oraxioms). It is in this way that philo-fiction creates not (once again) a linguistic fiction of another world yet to be described, but a universe-of-language, a universe-language each time, on the basis of the philo-world.

The subtracted-without-subtraction and subtraction

NP interprets "subtraction" by means of what it calls elsewhere "abasement" or depotentialization: the fall or "simplification" of transcendence, rather than the Hegelian "sublation" that continues to inspire Badiou, for whom "sublation" operates as "subtraction." To subtract in NP, all the same, is not a positive action of subtraction, or is more complex than that. The Real is both subtracted and subtraction, according to a "relation" of unilateral duality. To subtract without withdrawing into oneself and without exiting (from oneself) to go capture a prey, but instead to subtract by superposing—this is the non-acting which, thus, does not act, but does however subtract from the symbolic the means of future action upon the latter. The Real unilateralizes philosophical duplicity and its division according to a duality that is not a division operated by that philosophical duplicity. The subtraction of the Real itself is already done (and is to be redone or resumed); it is already subtracted and resumed qua subtracted, but is not itself the object of an explicit operation of subtraction. On the other hand, it is philosophy that is subtracted already for "half" of itself (transcendence is subtracted from its own doublet) because of its desire for the Real.

To subtract transcendence from its own doublet so as to replace it in immanence is not an action or a passion. It obviously has no subject or object at its extremities, just the Real of immanence and the world of transcendence. It is the non-acting of radical immanence, that which manifests the *means-to* any acting that would be valid for and in all possible worlds. Here, philosophy falls with one blow—*in its haste, it had forgotten to "produce" or to "manifest" according to the Real the means of all action or passion* (the "means of existence" as Marx says), to "engender" the mediate-without-mediation or the organon of immanence. A more fatal forgetting than that of Being, one which again drowns the Real in the world's circuit of exchanges, conflates the transformation of the world with the idealist regime of actions and passions, is complacent in its circles, totalities and encyclopedias, folds back on itself, its texts and its *villageoise* conservative mores. Thus begins that interminable drift, agony or survival called philosophy.

But if the Real does not act but nevertheless makes philosophy fall out of itself, there is subtraction at and from the point of view of philosophy in itself and for itself. Obviously, in this operation, philosophy, from its own point of view, far from seizing or capturing the Real (what, in reality, it wants to do) feels itself rather to be captured by it, possibly fascinated by and drawn toward it. But the correct "conversion" is to place oneself in the Real or in immanence via superposition or revival, and to uni-vert philosophy, to make philosophy fall. There are no other operations to carry out under the banner of a subtraction that is already virtually operative; it is simply a matter, on the basis of the philosophical occasion, of *taking the road towards the Real according to the Real.* Everything that is said here, for example, with regard to subtraction and NP, can always be read from within philosophical sufficiency, but it is all already operated virtually, not a first time but in prior-to-priority, and only necessitates the "second" stage of a resumption or of a superposition, rather than a repetition.

6

Philosophy and mathematics in the mirror

Philosophy and mathematics: A non-apparent specular couple

What is philosophy, what has it become and what should it be? *The response made implicitly to this question through the sole fact of posing it, is precisely what we call philosophy.* We live under this sometimes oppressive law of imaginary repetition without really having at our disposal any more rigorous notion of this fate. The most lucid thinkers of the preceding century, particularly those who addressed the historical mechanisms of this thought, only deepened them by repeating them more subtly or by displacing them. We are apparently very far from all doxa, but its "intellectual" (that is to say cultural) mediatization and globalization are once again a revelation of its anarchic nature—that is to say, its affinity with capitalism. Once, it was torn from doxa and laboriously distinguished from sophistry; must there be a second Platonic effort so as to raise it up again? To put it once more on an entirely mathematical terrain (not its original terrain, which was instead physical) is to prolong a glorious servitude. Badiou's additional step backwards, despite its brilliant realization, is not an objective observation of the success of philosophy, but a way of endorsing its failures. It would be better to stop treating philosophy philosophically in the spirit or in imitation of a mathematics superior to the transcendental itself, and sufficient; to stop thinking every thing as philosophizable and learn to know it—that is to say, to "materialize" once and for all (not even to rematerialize) its formalist and sufficient mechanisms and procedures.

Mathematics and Philosophy are twin sisters. The exaltation of one does not destroy the other, but stimulates it. Consequently (but this is obvious) it is impossible to contest in any way whatever the philosophy that draws assurance and sufficiency from seeing itself mirrored in mathematics. One can circle around the latter as around an Idea, it even can be considered *as* an Idea, but it is impossible to really penetrate into it—it is possible only to deprive it of its ontological part. Which may be to say either that philosophy is under mathematical condition, or that mathematics arrogates to itself a part of the work of philosophy—but in any case, they have a community of existence. We dare not say a common root, but at least a common mirror. The two sides are mirrored one in the other. We conclude that specularity is never simple or thing-oriented [*chosal*], but always bilateral, doubly specular, which initiates all consistency. This is the whole problem with the type of consistency of the set mathematics + logic + philosophy, along with the subject that is situated between each of these terms, if one does not rediscover the ancient tripartite logic/physics/ethics. This differentiated *chorismos*, this juxtaposition, has only an irreal consistency, a consistency through reciprocal reflections. What can hold them together, if not the mirror that is the Moebian torsion and its infinite doublets? Specifically, the coalition of a materialist position as philosophically absolute, and the installation within this space of a transcendental apparatus. Instead of being at the service of an absolute idealism, as in Hegel, it is placed in the service of materialism, and thus circulates between sciences, to the point of a quasi-procession of the Idea across this transcendental apparatus. "Materialist dialectic"—a materialist position as frame and a transcendental apparatus in the guise of a descendent dialectic.

The efforts to repress the One decidedly further, to as marginal a position as possible (as always, after having proclaimed its assassination, it is re-established) have some technical merit. And indeed, as to the One that accompanies Being as its twin, it was useful and fruitful to get rid of it, to distribute otherwise all these doublets. But OV only distends them, placing specular relations between them—even if it means recuperating in one way or another all these fragments of a chance partition, separated in advance. In place of these mathematico-imaginary relations, NP certainly has at its disposal what will be called (a little too simply) the One, to struggle against Heidegger and his primacy of Being; and then the One-in-One, to signify that it is a problem of immanence and not of "logical identity." But it was not a question of saying that radical immanence is a *subjectum*, a "total" or all-encompassing element, an undifferentiated "il y a," the grey or black indifferentiation that philosophers have made the preserve of bovines. To really allow these elements to "take," tearing them from philosophy and making them enter into the human kingdom of the generic, what is needed is the "precipitation" operated by the thought comprised within quantum physics.

In general, one can say that philosophy and mathematics are Siamese twins; that they must be separated and their mixing prevented (this mixing is called the transcendental, conjugating Plato, Kant and Heidegger), but that one of them can do nothing for the other except for prolonging their concord and their vast complicity, which is still exercised or tested by Badiou. Their whole is sterile and specular. One must seek reasons for the affinity between the axioms of infinity and pure philosophy as systematic compossibility. Philosophy still saves the traditional setting, despite this set-theoretical materialism. Affirming its void existence is all that remains to it; that is all it can still manage—just a sterile existence as guardian or superego of generic knowledges. The affirmation of the pure void and stellar transcendence replaces a too-present God. Classical physics introduces a beginning of the critique of philosophy (Kant), but it needed quantum theory to go further, for the physical grip on philosophy to attain its full potency.

The supposed mirror and the placing of philosophy into the matrix

Philosophy is a thought which, classically, is carried out with the help of a mediation—classically, the mirror of sense or of the signified, for the postmoderns the mirror of language and the signifier, and finally in the moderns the mirror of a science, logic, and then recently mathematics. In the mirror, accompanying it like a machine, is thus an image reflected in another element or organon which is most times logico-linguistic, thought more or less scientifically, and through which it entertains a specular relation of reflection with itself. It is thus a thought that we suppose to be "one" but which is divided with itself by that instrument of the mirror, and condemned to return to itself, to re-identify with itself or with its image, gaining by this identi-fication with science a supplement of consistency. This is the mirror stage, but generalized beyond individual psychology, since it includes in the "subject" science, along with language, insofar as they identify with themselves in the mirror. Now, it is capital to grasp that *the mirror is already a machine, a knowing machine, even; a machine of knowledge essential for philosophy and not just an instrument of its frivolity*. The mirror is a lying science *par excellence* because it touches closest to the truth. Doubtless a simple and sterile technology, an intention of void knowing and knowing to be voided, and which perhaps trans-forms the perceiving subject but not the thing perceived, it gives an interpretation of the world or an image of philosophy, but it is not its transformation. To break the image of thought qua image requires means entirely other than the philosophical, perhaps even mathematical means; for if the mirror is a knowledge or plays the part of a knowledge, it indeed takes the place of science in philosophy, giving it this possibility of speculation; but it is a usurped, or in any case premature, science. What have we done? Put philosophy in the matrix, deployed it in a form that takes seriously the clandestine function of the mirror and makes appear the customary dualities, the dualities of intervention, of science and of itself. Philosophy and science each intervene twice: the first time as object in discourse, and the second time as means or intention of a knowing.

Non-philosophy cannot be a reflection on a reflection, like a metaphysics of metaphysics. In that case one would get nowhere; in fact, one would lose everything. It has to use another principle—a scientific, not specular, mediation—even if it must still apparently intervene twice in the matrix, albeit in a non-specular manner. Now, the matrix in its OV version supposes that science (mathematics) intervenes as a mirror capturing ontology. We must thus change our means into functions of the scientific organon or the organon of mediation, not into those of the objects treated (we must not change one logic for another, one language for another). We must abandon it for an organon of another type, active and productive of knowledges—the mathematics whose genius is, as mirror, already to be partly linked with the linguistic context in the hands of philosophy, and, moreover, to be able to simulate science. What to do?

The non-philosophical version of the matrix will still utilize language and science, but will no longer reflect itself in them.

Since at least one productive science is necessary, we substitute another organon for the mirror, a full and non-specular science that will be able to extract philosophy from its narcissistic images of itself (PSP). But which science? Mathematics seems impossible to us, precisely because it maintains only specular relations with philosophy, their being like twin sisters who reinforce each other as sufficient, but without really transforming each other at all. Thus we will exclude it, and with it the Principle of Sufficient Mathematics (PSM). Philosophy does not transform mathematics but only the lived of mathematics; mathematics does not transform philosophy in its transcendental essence but only in its most external pretentions. Let us test another model of a possible organon: physics, and in particular, quantum physics. Physics because there is a materiality of immaterial concepts, of sense and even of the signified (and not only of the signifier); a body or a thickness of philosophy, innumerable geometric "metaphors," effects that, without being "material" in the sense of classical physics, have a materiality. This materiality resides in its effects, but is unperceived in the logico-linguistic mirror that deconstruction began to aim at, even as it limited itself to its textual and ultimately linguistic materiality. This will not therefore be a textual deconstruction left to the initiative of linguistics combined with the effect of Judaic transcendence.

If the secret of philosophy resides in this duality, this double requisition that the matrix brings out, then on this basis there are two solutions, not inverse but asymmetrical. Both contain the kernel of these two variables, language and science, and their relations, but also a doubling of one of them as factor, which puts their relations under condition. (We must remark that this matrixial posing of the problem will certainly not solve in the same way the problem that Quine posed in a too-classical and limited manner, the problem of the indetermination or the underdetermination of theory by experience. Augmenting and complexifying the variables, we cannot be content with saying that "experience" is insufficient to fully determine theory.)

A first solution will be proposed, then, as the fusion of language and science under language, as linguistic determination of their relations. This doubling of language, which returns on itself or closes itself, is philosophy itself as the most complete classical stance of thought. It could possibly be philosophy of science (nothing prevents this) but the latter, placing science in the servitude of the unity of philosophy, dominates it and transforms it into a mere mirror of philosophy—even the most well-armed science ends up being a mirror for philosophy. Language's self-relation is mediatized by a void mirror. Our thesis is thus that there must always be a mediation between philosophy and itself, and that the mirror plays this role, a mirror more or less full of one or many concrete scientific images.

The second solution is NP as unity of fusion of language and science, this time under science: it puts the relation of variables under a new type of condition that affects language in particular (but not exclusively). What does science become then? It is still partially, but secondarily, a mirror of philosophy; but it conserves its materiality intact, so that this materiality under-determines as such, in dominant manner, the fusion of variables. As far as mathematics is concerned, its materiality is too weak, and it becomes reabsorbed into the functions of the dominant mirror and of non-determination. In the case of physics, however—whose materiality is strong, and exceeds the specular—it underdetermines the fusion of variables.

If this matrix is in general valid, up to the permutation of factors, for philosophy and non-philosophy, then how do things stand with OV? OV is a mixed solution, where science is indeed a condition or factor, but as mathematical mirror; and it is philosophy, ultimately, that brings it in. The mathematical mirror is indeed an intention of science that has no need of quantum superposition, but which uses reflection as a philosophical-type "superposition," substituting this for its quantum form. It is a mixed solution that associates the philosophical with the mathematical part of quantum theory. We have found it necessary to limit the function and pertinence of mathematics to make room for quantum theory. The combination philosophy/science is the universal law, in any case, whether philosophy obeys a matrix but with the mirror of the mathematical, or not (transcendental unity, philosophy of science), and indeed whether or not the matrix is underdetermined by physics.

In OV, the scientific condition is not determinant, since it is, in fact, a matter of a mirror, albeit that of mathematics; and a mirror, let us repeat, is only valid for the subject that is reflected in it. Whence OV's characteristic sterility—indeed, its whole rigor consists in the bitter pursuit of that sterility. This is what opposes void (albeit generic) materialism, a philosophico-generic mixture, to the generic materiality without materialism

to which NP reduces philosophy or into which it transforms
it—what we call the "material formalism." Must we conclude
that mathematical ontology is a deceptive ontology, since it
is founded on a mirror [*miroir*] and a dazzling [*mirobolante*]
practice? If the mirror is the science of Master philosophers, all
that remains to them is to look good in it and to demonstrate
their true mastery—a technical mastery. Badiou does not fail to
do so, and rather twice than just one time.

It is the whole materialist theory of reflection, of knowledge
as reflection and its ambiguity, that must be explored by placing
it into the matrix. It says that it works through reflection,
but that it is ultimately (in the last instance?) a reflection of
matter. This is already an advanced materialist thesis, but
for NP knowledge is material in itself; it is only partially a
reflection in the mirror of philosophy, but not yet that of
matter. It is instead philosophy that would be a "decoherent"
(as quantum physics says) reflection in-the-last-instance of
non-philosophical materiality. The idealist or ideal conception
of knowledge and its rationalism cannot be projected onto the
materialist thesis, as if a materialist thesis could philosophically engender this rationalism. Perhaps one could say that
ideal knowledge or rationalism is a form of decoherence of
materiality or of material formalism; one would in this way
understand that quantum mechanics is the science of classical
physics, that the latter is its true object (a thesis we have always
maintained); just as generic quantum theory would be the
science of classical rationalism, as illustrated by the philosophy
of empirical sciences.

Getting out of the mirror: The hypothesis of a generic mathematics-fiction

Philo-fiction, because of the epistemological material that is our Old Testament, and because of the function that mathematics plays in it by way of quantum theory, must also be able to be a mathematics-fiction. At least, we could propose this hypothesis without knowing whether it is possible to make it happen or whether it is an excessive and unviable fiction. This is the meaning of a return from a supposedly divine mathematics to a human or generic mathematics, from the matheme to ante-mathematical mathesis, a prior-to-priority that must itself also be a disenchanted messianism reducible to discovery and invention. More exactly, NP puts into play, if not a correlation, at least a unilateral complementarity, mathesis-matheme, that can be understood as a "quantum machine"—a concept that makes little or no sense in terms of quantum physics, but only in terms of a quantum theory of philosophy, or NP. It is important to decompose into a unilateral duality the unitary mass of mathematics, constructed on the positivist and doubly transcendent privilege of the matheme, and which Badiou, among other philosophers, systematically exploits. No return here to the philosophical subject—mathesis is strictly speaking generic subject and undulatory-lived in the Last Instance. As to the particulate matheme, it would be the mathematical statement included in the immanence of mathesis, and would obviously see its power diminish—it would be depotentialized. Unilateral complementarities of this type are capable of a certain form of non-unitary uni-fication, of a human-and-mathetic "en-semblism" [*"en-semblisme"*],[1] not articulated in terms of exchanges, convertibilities, equivalences, etc. We shall call "en-sembles" masses or aggregates of unilateral complementarities or matheses-mathemes—unilations that are fabricated only from their extremities, insofar as they touch the world and draw from the physical world their occasional material. The mathetic root as "radical origin of things" is strictly unilateral, and exhibits a messianity that captures constituted mathematics. In reality, mathematics is human, and not at all divine—or it is divine only in man, not in God. But what is proper to philosophy is to conflate the root of the Last Instance with unity or foundation, to disperse it little by little or to ramify it into branches and leaves. It is in thus plunging toward the world that generic humans bind themselves, chain themselves, find themselves within an inextricable and harassing fabric, society or history, the Principle of Sufficient Philosophy (PSP) or sufficient or encompassing mathematics (PSM).

To speak of the "en-semble," of a unique immanence or state vector valid for all empirical (including mathematical) "sets," is to play with the genius of ordinary (that is to say, philosophized or philosophizable) scientific language, which one thus takes as an object of dualysis, interpreting it non-mathematically via the procedure of superposition or generic "re-quantification." The science of Man thinks it as an indivisible or infrangible but duel particle. The en-semble here is a material particle, but one with theoretical or "conceptual" content. En-semblist theoretical machines are particles as frontal or unifacial alterities. Doubtless they are two-headed, like desiring machines (Deleuze), but one head is a virtual flux of uni-rectional and indiscernible flux, the other a front or a frontal but immanent transcendence—the way in which radical immanence can "face" the world. On the contrary, a philosophical machine is made of at least two elements, but supposes always a third, which is the *homo ex machina*—he who takes the machine in hand and gives it its transcendent(al) human finality. This instance of mediation is more or less visible-hidden, and renders the other two visible. In the particulate or quantum machine, there are only two terms (it is radical), because the fundamental "term" or immanence is Man, who is that infrangible and invisible power of the particle in its trajectory. This is the unilateral en-semble, the one that is written with only one parenthesis, *One* (*Two*, and not with two parentheses as in unitary set-theoreticism (the transfinite). The en-semblist particle is an identity-without-unity, armed with a kinetic moment that speaks in terms of the half, or even the quarter, or the square root of -1 (the imaginary or complex number). En-semblism is more than dis-objectivating (and thus more than dis-alienating), because in reality it under-deter-mines or unijectivates the set. A phenomenology of unilateral complementarities thus emits a whole ante-Platonic mathesis. Philo-fiction will take the path of a *mathematics-fiction creative of unilateral or uni-jective complementarities and of their prior-to-priority over surobjectivated idealities.* As always, that which is emitted by dualysis as ante-Platonic will be revealed to be the effect of a human non-acting. A thought of the semblant is thus possible, but it will be that of the En-semblant or the One-in-One-(of the)-Semblant. The fundamental concept of set is thus recast and reemployed in the "fictional" style of a *non-mathematical en-semblism*, an en-semblism without calculation. It is an hypothesis.

Genealogy of the ontological-mathematical decision

The two elementary forms of philosophical space, immanence and transcendence, are apparently symmetrical, and equally abstract, in the sense that one cannot be isolated from the other. But the problem is that of the balance or the possible exchange between the two idioms. It is impossible to autonomize a pure immanence ("radical immanence" is not "pure") outside of all relation, at least all unilateralizing relation to the transcendence of Being; to distinguish it *absolutely* from the world that would then be a simple irreal. We will thus distinguish the absolute immanence that forms a mixture with transcendence and the bearer of appearance, from the radical immanence that can always contain "some" transcendence, or configure a particular moment without forming a mixture with it (but only a "unilateral complementarity"). As to the transcendence of decision, there is a pure or absolute transcending of decision that is its law and its Ideal, an operation in the form of a doubling or repetition, a doublet, a constitutive tendency of philosophy and one that tries to contaminate immanence in turn. But there is no repetition or doublet of immanence—its superposition, its "resumption," will be something entirely other. On the other hand, for transcendence, there is necessarily a repetition. The two elements of philosophy do not play at the same game and do not have the same "destiny" (Kant).

Given the mixed structure of this space of philosophy—immanence and transcendence, but also identity and difference, the internal and alterity—two extreme and apparently symmetrical solutions can be made, which attempt to dismember or to break this mixture through another organization that makes use of unilaterality. One consists in reducing the Real to immanence alone, and thus to the One-of-the-last-instance, but on condition of transforming its concept and of describing a non-decisional and non-positional, but instead superpositional, immanence-(of)-self. This solution is NP; it is the generic, not merely philosophical or epistemological, thinking of science. The other solution consists, on the contrary, of reducing the Real to transcendence alone, and thus to Being, on condition here again of modifying its concept, of rendering it absolute, or of thinking it as multiple and then as the void which, in a certain way, posits and names itself—this is OV.

Transcending remains (this is an essential law) relative to that which it surpasses, even when it is carried to the absolute or to the void, and even when it knows nothing of its origin, except perhaps to reduce it to a void philosophy of the Void. Now, this relative transcending is precisely none other than philosophical decision itself. Which explains why OV necessarily continues, or is duplicated in, a philosophy under the new name, which rather

betrays this continuity, of "meta-ontology"; and in the traditional form of an affinity (or a privilege) between a particular
science *and* the philosophical (here baptized "ontological"). We
have elsewhere isolated under the name of the "idealist triad"
the classical schema of the idealist appropriation of science by
philosophy. Here it is played out again: (1) A particular science,
or even a particular theory, is extracted from the continuum
of constituted knowledge and abstracted from its process of
production (here, axiomatized set theory); (2) It is identified with
a science universalized as the very essence of science ("mathematics" as paradigm); (3) Finally, the latter, through a simple
supplement of universalization, is identified with ontological
knowledge, the most essential of all knowledges, that of being
itself qua being. That the knowledge that constitutes, so to
speak, the basis of philosophy, should be of a nature other than
philosophical, and that Being curiously escapes the legislation of
the philosopher—here is an objective appearance that must be
penetrated in order to render to philosophy and to science their
respective dues, and to abandon these attempts at their absolute
de-suturation and their relative suture. All such attempts are
founded on the middle-term of a particular science and on the
operation of its philosophical appropriation—even when, as is
the case here, the philosophical intervention discovers a way to
render itself imperceptible.

This miraculous vanishing is possible thanks to that which
philosophy and mathematics have in common: transcending,
decision, which permits this amphiboly of the foundational
equation mathematics = ontology. From our point of view,

this is to say that a really pure and absolute transcending is not possible, or is only an appearance; that it is always fulfilled and co-determined by a relative decision; but that transcending is *par excellence* that which, belonging at once to science (to mathematics, to its idealities) and to philosophy, can be interpreted ambiguously and can give the appearance, in particular, that it is really and only absolute. This appearance is born of the conjunction of the always initially relative decision of the philosophical and the ideal decision of mathematics: their intersection produces the objective appearance of a really absolute (that is to say, real or ontological) decision; but as if it were *purely* ontological and entirely disburdened of the finitude of philosophical decision. The equation mathematics = ontology is thus nothing but an auto-negation of decision. Whence also the general style of the miracle, of the conjuncture achieved without any real work, that belongs to this contemplative thought. On the one hand, the modern pathos of the operation in general is not present only for the one (the operatory transparency of the count-for-one); but also for being (subtraction, presentation). It blossoms with the concepts of structure and law, of meta-structure and the operation of operation; of the formalized axiomatic. The operatory style—that of deductive effectiveness—is substituted for that of the phenomenon in ontology. Phenomenological metaphysics is inverted/displaced, or referred back to an axiomatic practice of number or of calculation. In any case, the operatory style is but a half of the essential relation; there is also the side of being and of the void. But these two sides—the void and the operatory transparency of the count—have in common, as we have said, that they are both modes of transcending. The operation, the count, the operation of the count—the calculation that, in this ontology, is supposed to replace philosophical decision—touches the void through the transparency of its inessentiality. To calculate before philosophizing, and so as to be able to philosophize, is possible only if calculation—the symbolic manipulation of the letter—is, after all, "in direct contact" with being, which in turn is possible only if being is a void or a pure transcending. Calculation represents the transcendence of ideality, being the pure transcending that is the void of denumerable idealities; but the transcendence of mathematical ideality is already no longer relative to the empirical.

The most important part of our problem is that amphiboly implied by the concept of "transcendence," or, more exactly, every form of thought that makes use of it in a "first" or philosophical manner. It is this amphiboly that must be elucidated as to its ultimate root. This is only possible if we already possess two *radically* heterogeneous concepts of transcendence, and if, on this basis, we can discern how they are confused in a unitary appearance, the appearance that is at the basis of this mathematical materialism. It is one (one only, but a fundamental one) of the objects of NP to distinguish these two concepts as crucially as possible; which it does by dissociating or "dualysing," on the basis of the One understood as vision-in-One: (1) a transcendence free of all decision, a priori real of the latter, what we have elsewhere called "non-decisional or non-thetic Transcendence (NTT)," and which we now call, in the new quantum context, "particulate transcendence" or "fallen into-immanence"; (2) the philosophical form or forms of transcendence or of alterity—the latter serving as mere "occasion" for the former. The mechanism of objective unitary appearance is simple and, without itself being miraculous (it is a doubling or a doublet), it produces the miraculous appearance of an always already operated unity (it is thus after the fact, after dualysis, that its miraculous nature appears) of these two concepts; a unity that is all of philosophy itself, its proper mysticism and fetishism, its theological quibbling (Marx). A genesis, in truth, that is solely ideal rather than real—it is not a question of really engendering the mixture of philosophical decision that is already given "pre-arranged," given as a symptom of the world.

This mechanism is as follows: in a sense, the non-thetic Transcending (contained as particulate noema in immanence, and which is radical or simple in its order) and the mixed transcending (always relative at the same time as absolute) of decision have nothing in common—apart from the unity of fact between the two, which is the point of view of philosophy itself. This two itself draws its ultimate essence from what we call unilateral duality (One-in-One + any other term whatsoever = X, for example a decision, a term that is contingent by and for the One). Now, it is enough that they should be two (for philosophy) for the transcendings to be confused, in its eyes, and for there to be a unity between them, for them to participate in a medium and representative generality. We see here that philosophy is inseparable from the linguistic and textual generalities that smooth over heterogeneity and which are unitary by definition—and that it tries to think the real through them. In the present case, even if these two experiences of transcending have nothing essential in common, philosophy cannot but seek their unity, their identity even. It does so with the sole means at its disposal, by going to the shortest or the lowest—this is its empiricism: it is the perceptive-linguistic form, the most general and the most unitary form of transcendence, that serves as a common measure or stock for the two forms of decision. *A fortiori* it serves as a median element for philosophy and ontologico-mathematics. Whence (for reasons that thus belong to philosophical-type thought itself, which is spontaneously amphibological) the amphiboly of those forms of transcendence that still nourish OV and its declarations of "purity." The purism of Badiou's neo-Maoism is nourished, as always, on dissimulated mixtures. To understand the special type of amphibology that belongs to OV—and, beyond this, the amphibological style of all philosophy—we shall turn our attention to those philosophico-linguistic generalities that fuel its discourse and that, above all, surreptitiously make possible its articulations or decisions—precisely decisions that tend to efface themselves in their very effectuation. For example, to the relation between being and presentation, responds the relation of the pure multiple to the count-for-one—they are probably at once the same relation and two distinct relations, one passing between being and its thought, the other between thought and itself. That is to say, the necessary amphiboly of the concept of "inconsistent multiplicity" or of "presentation in general," which assures the passage from being as void to consistent multiplicity. It points at once toward being as foreclosed to presentation and toward the presentation available to the count-for-one. It is the third term, or that which remains of it, that assures the unity (that is to say, the very existence) of the "relation" of being and knowledge, of the multiple and the one, etc. This concept is a sort of vanishing median term reduced to the bar of foreclosure insofar as it represses and unites. It is perhaps not only this double/unique function that still endows the relation multiple/one with its nature as undivided relation. The eviction of mediation or of the one-that-is does not leave two lonesome terms in pure indifferent juxtaposition; it leaves in place the residue of the very function of foreclosure (with the residual form of unity that belongs to it), and the term that fulfills this function in reality: that of "inconsistent multiplicity."

The philosophico-linguistic generalities of unitary function, which are freighted with reciprocity, needed to be limited "radically," along with their paradigm: the One-that-is. But they left a residue—for there is still, after all, something of the One; there is always more than we would like, and what is more it is the worst One, in the form of those mixed or intermediary beings that are charged with reconciling the spirit of non-reciprocity or unilaterality through the philosophical necessity of maintaining the primacy of relations (inconsistent multiplicity, meta-ontology, the "non-defined term"). Meta-ontology, in particular, makes a line or a passage between ontology and philosophy. It must (if not, what would philosophy be?) still be called (meta-) "ontology," and the abyss between mathematics and philosophy must be bridged somewhere. Meta-ontology is the foreclosure of (mathematical) ontology by philosophy, we might say, at the same time as its philosophical "expressibility" after all.

Without this continuity, which would have it that decision auto-anticipates itself under and in the form of mathematical ontology, it is hard to see how (if not through some additional miracle) philosophy could welcome ontologico-mathematics, and the other generic procedures; how it could be affected by the latter and organize their compossibility. That is to say, the rigor of OV in the positing of the multiple is, as always, more heroic than real. For these philosophico-linguistic generalities, in their turn, dissolve the virulence of the multiple. "Presentation in general" or "inconsistency" (between consistency and the void) strongly risks once more crushing the pure multiplicities that it is charged with speaking. Natural language, in its philosophical usage, already overly pervades mathematical ontology (qua ontology not qua mathematics). And it is all of philosophy, all of the reciprocity of the One and of Being, that re-turns in this way—the return of the One...

The extent to which OV remains within decision is confirmed by the fact that ontology reverses (*Being and Event* tells us it is "a reversal") the initial state of the being of consistency and inconsistency:

> their primitive consistency is prohibited by the axiom system, which is to say it is ontologically inconsistent, whilst their inconsistency (their pure presentative multiplicity) is authorized as ontologically consistent.[...]

Ontology, axiom system of the particular inconsistency of multiplicities, seizes the in-itself of the multiple by forming into consistency all inconsistency and forming into inconsistency all consistency. It thereby deconstructs any one-effect; it is faithful to the non-being of the one, so as to unfold, without explicit nomination, the regulated game of the multiple such that it is none other than the absolute form of presentation, thus the mode in which being proposes itself to any access.[2]

What does it mean to say that the absolute transcending includes surreptitiously within it a decision that sustains its existence? That the pure decision that makes the void (of) being qua being is impregnated with a decision every bit as relative as that with which traditional philosophy begins? This necessary connection of absolute or mathematical ontology and the philosophical is the symptom of another relation, yet more essential: that of all transcendence (even supposedly pure or void) to immanence, which always conveys decision; the necessary reference of Being to the One, even as presence, and the force of their mixture. The equation mathematics = ontology is obviously of a piece with the axiom "the One is not." We must cut down (or believe that we have cut down) the One, that of metaphysics or that of philosophy, to thus free or believe ourselves to have freed transcending or Being (that of ontology). If philosophy has always been an intrication of Being and the One (according to variable proportions and relations, all of which however respect this invariant), and if a decision in the last resort supports absolute mathematical being, then immanence in the last resort supports this apparently absolute transcending. Hence the axiom: "the one is not" (understood in the sense that OV takes it, for it remains ambiguous, and many philosophies or mysticisms assume its literal truth), which is necessary so that Being can be, or be absolute, remains surreptitiously conditioned by the One—that is to say, by the One-that-is of presence or of metaphysics—by what we call decision. The vain rage to cut everywhere, to partition so as to better organize, to put in battle order—such is the ethos and the pathos of Badiou the Maoist.

The empty set and the transcendental

Badiou wanted to save definitively the old ontical materialism, by transforming it into ontological materialism; by putting ontological intelligibility into mathematics, or vice versa. This "ontology" of the void signifies a materialism without matter, a materialism possessing its own proper intelligibility which is ultimately philosophical.

In what way is materialism in general subtractive in relation to idealist presence? It is in general subtractive in relation to the doubled One or the divided One of idealism—it is its impoverishment or its slimming-down—but it still supposes it in this reduced form, or at least affects to be able to deny it with the same facility that it denies the unit-of-the-count. So what is the status of the empty set? Is this One not conserved as One, obviously no longer that of calculation but that of the *set-form as such, in the empty set which is always, however empty, at least full of its form*? And how could form—even void form—not be a tributary of the most idealist One? Badiou has certainly examined this problem. Will not the identification of the void and the One be the substrate or the condition of that of the void and of Being?

Against the idealist auto-projection of the One, NP for its part argues for the One-in-One or non-projective, non-ecstatic or semi-ecstatic immanence. As for OV, it argues for the supposedly non-projective *transcendence* of the One as simple unit-of-the count. It refuses, rightly, the doubling and the projection of the One, and makes a non-projective but "flat" and mathematical ontology, rather than one centered on immanence via quantum superposition, as NP does. But matter (the multiple) must be able to have or to receive the form of the simple One, the set-form; and what is more it must be able to contain the possibility of the subtractive, which is thus the empty set, *the form-One as void or the One that is subtracted from the doubled One*. The paradox or the wager of OV lies in this syntagm of the "empty set" that appears contradictory *on the ontological plane*. The materialist knowledge of the multiple will contain its own principle, which is the void and its subtractive power, with the duplicity of presence. The risk, if there is one, is that of a transcendental flattened onto itself. Does Badiou not presuppose a simplified transcendental as organon vested in the matter of the mathematical multiple? *The empty set is the universal denuded of all qualities, a hyperstructural transcendental—Badiou supposing, moreover, that what is called "the transcendental" is the same thing as Idealism*, whereas it is in no way anything more than that part of ideality necessary to every philosophy or ontology, even a materialist one. Whence its necessary future "return" to center stage.

Materialism seems however to have need of a philosophy to double mathematical ontology and to draw out the truths of generic ontology. An explicit, evacuated doubling returns here: in entrusting ontology to mathematical science, materialism obliges itself to require a meta-ontologist philosopher, the philosopher benefitting from a last power which is that of metalanguage as structural or constitutive. Whereas NP deconstructs the duplicity of transcendence or the projection of the One—so that there will no longer be a philosopher *ex machina* to once again double, after all, the form-One-of-the-set. More exactly, so that, if there is always a certain subject *ex machina*, it should at least be clearly recognized as such, and not dissimulated, as philosophers often do through their own actions. The enterprise that goes by the name of physics and above all of quantum duality, which admits clearly a subject or an experimenting agent, is from this point of view less contradictory or duplicitous than the enterprise put under the tutelage of mathematics, which, as we see, once again ceaselessly mirrors itself in philosophy. Having wished to annul the mirror of the transcendental as auto-projection by flattening itself upon itself, it rediscovers it later on, and is incapable of truly escaping it. And this is the basic dilemma of the empty set as ontology: its existence only multiplies the specular effects and extends them into the whole edifice. *Logic of Worlds*, from this point of view, is a supplementary level added to this fortress and its battlements so as to consolidate it.

The purism of mathematico-ontological decision

The outcome of Badiou's problematic is particularly meager: on the mathematical side, we have the empty set; on the philosophical side, the equally empty category of truth; and between the two, the subject, on the edge of the void. Nothing is left, just traces of footsteps in a desert. It could be that, rather than harboring mirages, it is the desert itself that is a mirage drawing Badiou onward. But no matter. The true content of his oeuvre is that of a mathematician and a writer, but one of no great philosophical flesh or sensibility. It is not surprising that the transcendental reappears once more *in extremis*. Platonism is the sphere of the *mathemata* qua knowledge that one is taught but that one already possessed a priori, in the hands of a transcendental will that is philosophy. This articulation does not appear in the form of the Kantian subject but in the form of a meta-ontology that has the transcendental as its destination in any case, which will be confirmed in what follows. The classical transcendental as synthesis is leveled by the materialism of the void, for it cannot fail to reappear owing to the very fact of the twin-ness of mathematics and philosophy within the *mathemata*. Badiou holds at a distance the two disciplines, while widening their hiatus, and even that between generic truths and void philosophy, whereas on this point, Plato is the first to mix them and to run into "disaster." Ultimately, there is a *transcendental void* that enables communication between the generic and philosophy (which, in itself, is no longer transcendental).

To submit philosophy to science, OV and NP both begin with a scientific form, but one that is ontologically and/or philosophically interpreted. In one case, Pythagoreanism unifies the Platonic Idea and the mathematical set; in the other, generic quantum theory unifies the One-in-One and the algebraic form of idempotence (radical immanence as strong-analytic and weak-synthetic). OV posits that the set-form is emptied of beings by subtraction, but not empty of Being. NP begins with algebraic idempotence, which is void of Being and beings, of ontological Difference itself, because it is full of immanence by superposition, full of the One-in-One. We have either Being as the empty set, or the same as idempotence. The latter can be deduced from set-theoretical properties, no doubt (as Badiou objects to Deleuze, the fold, disjunction, flux etc., are all reducible to set theory). But this is to suppose that set theory is decided upon as foundational theory of mathematics, which is already a problematic decision; and what is more, that ontology is fundamental (not in Heidegger's sense)—a philosophical, not mathematical, thesis. A double game, playing on the deductive capacity of set theory and on its "genealogical" capacity, which assures the authority of this initial position. In reality, these decisions are contingent, or belong to tradition. Where does this privilege of the set-form come from, if not from an interpretation of set theory—one that is already secretly philosophical, and thus vicious. *Is this the source of the ontological identity of the set itself, which is maintained even in the case of the empty set?* Badiou seems to forget about this, because, as a materialist and positivist in his own way, it is the matter of the void or of zero that interests him for all reality. In short, the equation "mathematics = ontology" is one of those miraculous encounters to which philosophy holds the secret. Which is no big deal—it is enough to recognize it, and not to become stubbornly dogmatic about it. What is important is that, to present the double Platonico-Aristotelian dimension of philosophy as science and as doxa, requires a complex formula that conjugates (but very prudently, not spontaneously) *some* science and *some* philosophy. Science must be the under-determining (but in the last instance) and not merely the subtractive condition here; not merely the condition that is content to void philosophy of its myths and its beings. Science must penetrate into philosophy, under-determine it, no doubt, and to this end fuse with it or be superposed with it. Mathematics with the empty set keeps too much of a distance from philosophy, and is content to void it of its content without changing or transforming it. The purism of the mathematical foundation, albeit subtractive, has no real hold over philosophy. The beginning itself must be mathematico-logical, Platonico-Aristotelian, that is to say endowed with the universal force of algebra, capable of taking on philosophy in its entirety, and not merely purifying the ancient myth within/of it. OV is ideal philosophy, or more precisely the Ideal of philosophy, that forgets the ideal philosophies that are constituted in it and against which it struggles, in the void. Could we not imagine instead a politics that would be rather less ascetic but more widely combative against the philosophy-all? Marx, with his breadth of vision and horizon, is betrayed by Badiou, who brings together a mathematicizing materialism and an empty philosophy that is but the purified dogmatism of the militant. The science of philosophy would better begin as an algebra of philosophy, and be realized as a quantum theory of its materiality.

7

Ontology and materiality

The undulatory turn and philosophical materiality

The question of conceptual style generally comes down to the critique of representation or of presence, which are far from having come to an end. How to be able to conceive of them in terms of the primacy of mathematics as void? We should have to accept the passage to a physics of philosophical bodies. As scientific models to introduce into thought, we oppose globally the philosophical and the generic, but also set-theoreticism and particle physics, topological torsion and the undulatory turn, the macroscopic and classical style of Badiou and the quantum-undulatory style, set-theoreticism [*ensemblisme*] and en-semblism, with its dash that separates only to unify through superposition or through the "*in*-One" the semblant of philosophy. In physics there was an undulatory turn, which was decisive for the quantum conception, and whose effects have not yet been felt within philosophy. Badiou ceaselessly planifies, classes and orders, hierarchizes to the point of establishing a kind of materialist procession of the Idea, incarnated in a truth-body. The operations, instances, functions, strata or dualities are of a corpuscular rather than particulate style. Mathematics as model is directed predominantly by forms, and induces a quasi-mathematical form or formalism of philosophy qua macroscopic. The Idea of Plato and Pythagoras is a bifurcation or a possible solution, but there is another, which consists of upholding the specific materiality of philosophy or that of which it speaks. Geometrical and arithmetical formalism, more topological than algebraic, outlines a formal image: eidos and figure, idea as figure—here is true "presence," it is operatory and not solely thematic. To avoid formalism within philosophy and to return it to its materiality, the approach via the quantum of action is fundamental. Philosophical materiality consists in its effects upon science and those of science upon it, not only "effective philosophy," which remains largely auto-referential and under PSP. Certain Marxists evoke a materiality of ideology, a productive force of the idea—this is not a matter of a sensible materiality of concepts or of intuition accessible to sense, but of a materiality of effects emitted or regulated by a quantum or a minimum packet. The effects may be conceptual or may operate on the ideological level, but one must treat them as materials in themselves, sensible or intuitive materials. It is a matter of a wave function, but one of a neutralized lived that serves as law or rule for the effects. Perhaps one could speak also of quanta of affect or of action. Philosophy mobilizes algebra and topology, doubtless, but an algebra simply grasped within its own theory, outside any physical application or translation. To be exact, philosophical-style formalism is algebraic or operatory, but also topological, a formalism of placement. This is the mathematical and structuralist inspiration of Badiou, from *Theory of the Subject*[1] on. He projects philosophy, and even the Idea and Truth, onto calculations and spaces, rather than incarnating it immediately in a body. All deconstructions of presence, including the set-theoretical one, are enterprises of philosophy upon itself, and have no scientific status except a presupposed one.

Set-theoretical ontology—a new Schrödinger's cat

As to the conflictual status of the Multiple between Deleuze and Badiou, between Difference and the Cantorian multiple, we have seen that the quantum and generic point of view of the particulate multiple allows us to detect the presupposition of a decisional and differential transcendent conception, of the identity that is hidden in particularly subtle manner in OV.

The immediate identity of Being and the Set, albeit unilateral in the favor of the latter, is a particularly dogmatic thesis to the eyes of the philosophies of Difference, which

go on to object (Deleuze) that the authentic Multiple is not
that which is posited by subtractive opposition to the One,
but the becoming that passes from one multiple to another,
"between" two multiples. But equally, from NP's point of
view, mathematical ontology is a dogmatic, quasi-scientistic
thesis. Of course, it is inevitable that one allows oneself to
be given the real or that which holds its place, but the real of
this identity results from a simple abstraction-subtraction that
flattens Difference onto itself, leaving it flecked with unana-
lyzed and always active Presence—and, behind it, let us add,
the unimpaired authority of philosophy. This surtraction and
autotraction of transcendence is a magical thought *par excellence*, an unprecedented voluntarism (Badiou: "we are greater
than all gods," etc.)

If we wish to renounce the means of Difference without
returning to a dogmatism of transcendent construction, and
even less to the pseudo-thinking interiority of reflection,
there is no other solution than to let-be-given what we have
called the "vision-in-One," that is to say the affect-(of)-One or
(of)-radical immanence. This lived-(of)-identity "in" identity
is spoken of in quantum terms as "superposition," and not as
a simple "equation" mathematics = ontology. Strictly speaking,
this equation could be understood as a superposition no longer
operated in quantum terms. However, from the quantum point
of view, *a superposition whose terms remain transcendent and
macroscopic would be of the same type as Schrödinger's living-
and-dead cat.* Identity, yes, but via immanence rather than via
a transcendence that admits it to the dialectic. NP has never

opposed directly, under penalty of a return to the procedures of philosophy, the mathematical Multiple and the One itself in its transcendence. In reality, what we oppose to it (indirectly, on the basis of the One-in-the-last-instance) is radical immanence via the undulatory superposition of philosophy and science, with particulate becomings for each of them. There is a decisive difference between the identity of Being and of beings insofar as it is posited on the empirical basis of the latter or of their content (whence its precritical dogmatism and its merely truncated autopositional form, and complementarily, the negation of all identity that supports it and that it leaves unthought); or else on the basis of the One-in-the-last-instance—whence the critical sense of this "identity" and its non-autopositional form via the positive absence of all autoposition rather than via truncated autoposition.

We thus ask OV whence it draws this *surreptitious* identity that still conditions its concept of the multiple-as-void, and which it leaves unthought, limiting in the same stroke the non-consistency of this multiple "of" multiples, limiting it mathematically with a supposedly constitutive transcendent knowledge, when it would have been possible to free it by relating it to the Last Instance, which alone could explode the ultimate closures of the ontological or transcendent One. It is not because the ontology of the void claims the Multiple as Being that it frees its concept. It claims it too empirically or too immediately, it still founds its experience of Being upon a supposedly constitutive prior positive knowledge (mathematics), and falls back into the circle of empirical idealism.

A quantum or non-Cantorian ontology

With the vision-in-One, superposition or Last Instance, it becomes possible, far from "reducing" the Multiple to the metaphysical One, to free it in undulatory manner from its particulate and physical autonomy, into a universality more generic than its simple immediate and primary autoposition, which dissociates it between singularity on one hand and One-All or materialist thesis on the other. On the one hand, the One-in-the-last-instance renders intelligible as "interference" the form of identity still presupposed in any case by the Multiple, in some way clarifying its opacity from within, without suppressing it, without returning to a sterile and specular reflection. And on the other hand, it renders to the Multiple its relative or quantum-particulate autonomy that its primary or premature positing had restricted. It is obviously tough to tell the philosopher-hero for whom to think is to emerge from the head straight into the stars, to the un-bridled Platonist, that this hubris is not a liberation, that auto-decision or primary decision is not his greatest possible liberation but his self-confinement and his self-constraint; that only the quantum determination of the Multiple by the One-of-presence as generic superposition can liberate him from his ultimate mathematical or Cantorian closure, which is a mirror for philosophy. The refusal of the transcendent determinations of the Multiple or of the One-of-presence must be extended in the name of the Real via immanence, and no longer in the name of the real by excess or transcendence, to the point of its set-theoretical and Cantorian closure.

Let us not confuse the auto-destruction, the auto-inhibition of transcendence by itself or by militant excess, with its true liberation through a radical immanence that no longer confuses itself with this transcendence (it is no longer the system of Difference) any more than it reduces it. The great adversary, unsuspected by philosophers who seek thought in the excess of transcendence over itself and its putting into doublet, is the autoposition of the latter, and precisely in the excess of the "decision" that takes two symmetrical forms, the doublet or the flattened form, the ideal of planification. Nietzschean superposition was already a subtle mode of autoposition, a first reduction of the transcendent into transcendence. Excess as universal de-position manages to purify transcendence of its ontical determinations, to liberate Being from the particularity of beings, but it still does so only to confide it to Beings as their unsurpassable negative condition. Whence the blindness that produces an excess of stellar light, with no more "interiority" or "intimacy" than the unconscious; and its incapacity to find in this intimate experience-(of)-the-invisible the secret of the lived.

It may seem rather facile to announce, like Badiou, the death of the "god of the One." The means utilized, as we have seen, belong to a transcendent practice of thought that operates via arbitrary decision and abstraction. As for the (ultimately derisory) idea of the One that is proposed to us as the unit-of-the-count, this denigration is more ancient that one imagines, and has a sense other than that which he gives it. It is congenital to the philosophical stance, which cannot but repress the real-One and give it a now overly lofty, now too-diminutive image. Here, the

One is confused with an arithmetico-transcendental mixture. There is no deconstruction of a supposed reign of the One, there is but a short-sighted vision of the effect of the multiple. The reign of the One would suppose the government of Being, and it is this philosophical set that must be deconstructed. The convertibility of the One and Being, despite the thesis that "the One is not," remains undefeated by the new modern cut. The One-in-One itself, in Being, is undeconstructible via any philosophical operation. Instead, it permits a new usage of the cut, set-theoretical or otherwise, and of unilateral deconstruction as transformation. The One is not, this is true—but it alone can under-determine its knowing, without creating it from scratch.

The Deleuze case

With Deleuze's multiplicities, it is a matter neither of the Cantorian Multiple nor of its simple equalization with the One; there is no equation, no equality Multiple = One, nor, above all, ultimately any thesis on the One, as Badiou suggests there is. It is a matter of the One-All, or, strictly speaking, of the correlation of two theses: that of the molecular Multiple and that of the One. Despite this correlation, we cannot conclude that Deleuze is still a philosopher of the One in the heavily metaphysical sense in which Badiou intends the term. He denounces the One of multiplicities, despite the great simplification of transcendence to which Deleuze commits, with his plane of immanence. And he does it in the name of the Cantorian multiple of multiples. At first surprising, this interpretation has a certain justice, if only partial. The Deleuzian thesis of the One-All is accompanied by the adverse thesis on the Multiple. They are inseparable and must be thought together, but is there not a certain asymmetry between them, and a final privileging of the One-All, so that Badiou would finally have been right? But if he is right, and the objection to a generality and a cause certainly weighs above all against Deleuze, it weighs also against Badiou himself. Owing to an insufficiently profound analysis of double transcendence, and a naive and quasi-positive conception of philosophy, he posits this Cantorian multiple and then the void in a last reference to a One that is operatory in the matrix (as we have seen above), but which remains thematically unperceived by him. It cannot at all be confused with the unity-of-the-count with which he believes himself able easily to govern its count (as if it were possible to slice into a concept with the blade of the axiomatic axe) except, obviously, if one proceeds in quantum manner, by bringing the set of variables back into the materiality of the undulatory lived. Under the apparently non-consistent multiple, he conserves the absolute axiomatic act that he transfers to philosophy. We recognize in his multiple the inverted philosophical gesture, materialism. Badiou's multiple, once we examine the philosophy in its materiality and not as a simple positional materialism, is a return of the corpuscular One in the form of the void or specular zero, and in the form of the various holes with which he sprinkles his construction. Thus, we must refuse Deleuze and Badiou together, as decisions that are symmetrically opposed, but both wholly philosophical—replacing them with unilateral complementarity.

This said, Deleuze's problem perhaps lies in a type of fusion of the Multiple and the One, which remains a classical doubling via the body without organs. He did indeed try to simplify the doublet of transcendence into a "plane of immanence" that is less naive than the materialist thesis, but only by delivering it to a last, Moebian transcendence, an internal transcendence. It is hard to say whether the One must return a second time even for a Moebius band to secure and re-close the All. From our point of view, the "insufficiency" of his position would then lie in the transcendental type of fusion that the molecular and the logic of disjunction suppose. This is why, when it comes to this fusion, we instead use the quantum superposition of immanence proper to machines that we call "unilateral complementarity," and of which the generic matrix is the typical example.

Mathematics and ontology: From mirror to collision

If philosophy is put under mathematical condition, that is to say *deprived of its ontology*, without a calculative set-theoretical transcription being made of philosophy or even of the ontology that one cannot set-theorize, it would be very surprising if mathematics itself were not placed, at least, "under the influence" if not "under condition" of philosophy—that is to say, ultimately conceptualized or plunged into the mirror of language and sense. There is necessarily a dissymmetry from the outset between the two variables: a quasi-hermeneutics of set theory or of its axioms is possible, but there is no calculus of philosophical concepts. Thus, even if one admits the absolute autonomy of mathematical production, one must still *recognize* it with a meta-ontological decision that already exceeds the simple axiomatic of the infinite, so that the recognition of mathematics is in fact a veritable co-constitution. The clarification of these relations shows that philosophy is already operative within mathematical ontology, that philosophy is not only that structure of reception that awaits beyond ontology, but that it is engaged in the decision mathematics = ontology; that what we find here is only apparently an absolute given, and that this absolute thesis in fact dissimulates one relative decision among others, a decision that is contingent and thus not at all definitive. *It is the voluntarist style, that is to say the style of the miracle*, that Badiou, with these absolute theses, intends to introduce into philosophy—which obviously was ready to receive it. We must not let this type of dogmatic decision intimidate us (for that is what it is about). The actual infinite and mathematics require an act of positing, but one that effaces itself in the positing. When it is realized in the effectivity of an ontological thought, the actual infinite mutates into an absolute or in-doublet transcending, a philosophical Ideal, and must necessarily be affected by a decisional, and *presently transcendental*, limitation of this absoluteness. The attempt to distribute otherwise ontology and philosophy belongs to that constellation of the more-than-decision that founds thought upon the transcending of a pure void. Like every philosopher, Badiou makes adverse terms enter into duality, into an amphibological "collision"—one that is precisely not rethought as quantum collision—that is to say, one that proceeds without examination of the possibility of a product of a science by philosophy, or of a relative homogeneity of the genres of reality and materiality. If he had posed in quantum terms the problem of the superposition of mathematics and philosophy, he would then have been able to transfer the set of variables into a homogeneous materiality, that of the lived as the materiality of the generic subject or of the Last Instance. The philosophical collision is always of the order of the amphiboly or of the "bad fusion" of contraries, primary and "savage," rather than that of a quantum collision, for which the opposites would have been *prepared and not thrown brutally into the imaginary collider of philosophy—that is to say, into the mirror.* It is in fact always identity and the logic of identification that reigns, instead of superposition. In NP, *the supposed contraries are prepared, in the state of symptoms, and can then be treated in a true experiment, not in a specular game of things-in-themselves.* The brute collision (in fact entirely imaginary) of opposites in an identity is not their true collision—it is a dialectics and thus a sophistics, not a physics. The "dialectic" does not seem to us to be saved any more by materialism than by idealism, no more than is materiality. The paradox of NP as conceptual quantum theory is perhaps that it begins by multiplying reciprocally one by the other science and philosophy, seeming to abandon the rule of unilaterality; but it is a matter of rendering relatively homogeneous two factors that are otherwise incommensurable, except through the arbitrary or impossible leap of philosophy. And in any case this rule it is only partly surrendered—for we rediscover afterwards and "finally" the unilaterality that "inclines" the two inverted products toward the undulatory immanence of the Last Instance. Precisely, philosophy in its operations is ready to accept unilaterality as, for example, Difference, but in a precipitate manner that does not give it its full, extended domain of action.

The mechanism of amphiboly is still a compromise, a solution designed to dissimulate decision all the better to reproduce it, dissimulating it in mathematics and in the axiomatic that is supposedly capable of wresting ontology from philosophy, and rejecting the latter into its unitary and conjunctural functions, which only save it by amputating it from what was traditionally its principal part. One seems thereby to reduce philosophy but, in secreting this part of it within a science, one in fact saves philosophy, communicating to it indirectly this solidity or this would-be "definitive" solution to its problems. The absolute, more than-decisional partitioning of philosophy between that which is dead (Presence, to be absolutely interrupted) and that which is living or thinking (mathematics)—and this at the level of a prioris that structure and produce philosophical cognition—aims to withdraw decision from philosophy (it is sent back to mathematics, where it is effaced, at least as philosophical-type decision) and to leave it to its tasks (conservative tasks, moreover) of inventory and synthesis. The result is a half-solution: it diminishes the import of philosophy and its anti-scientific idealism; it holds up science as the absolute "basis" of philosophy; it associates in a second mirror the two adversaries that it believes thereby to remove from their perpetual war. It is a useful step, but it is still philosophy that advances here, masked by its identification/reabsorption into mathematics = ontology. A Marxist-inspired solution, no doubt, where science is introduced of itself, so it seems, into the aged edifice of philosophy, and occupies a defined place there. But this place ages too, precisely because what is specific to philosophy is, in any case, transcendence—relative and absolute, but primarily relative. That here it should be absolute, whilst still integrating the relative and semi-irreversibility—this solution does not destroy the usual relation of sufficient philosophy to science, it just "reverses" it once more. For suppose that science—on its mathematical side—develops in the void or in pure transcending, which is the true content of mathematic "ideality"; the operation of philosophy then traditionally consists in extracting this ideality and imprinting the decision-form on it; in folding/refolding it in the form of a transcendental and auto-positional *factum*, the Idea. Here we find traces of that operation, but in a more subtle form. For it is the Transcending of the pure Void which is thus refolded upon itself and which becomes the *factum* that founds the absolute theses. Only the fold is no longer seen—it is as if reabsorbed and effaced in itself precisely because the material of decision (that with which it is primitively identified) consisted of pure mathematics or of the void, rather than mathematico-sensible or empirico-ideal correlations such as those of physics. There is indeed a fold, but so perfectly realized, so little unfolded and rendered visible from the sensible and perceived exterior, that it is imperceptible from there; truly, this is the blind confidence of the philosopher-mathematician. Thus decision discovers the procedure, in mathematics, to erase its own footprints, its finitude, to efface itself and to render itself insensible; so that, thanks to this rare miracle, mathematics sets itself to speaking all at once and with an absolute clarity the logos that previous philosophers had only stammered out; and philosophy, finally, can now clothe itself with an air of innocence and receive science with a welcome to which its sufficiency and its traditionally hegemonic comportment had not habituated us.

If philosophy thus persists at the heart of mathematical ontology, what is left of it now? What can it do as philosophy, deprived of its most important working part? The equation mathematics = ontology, through its immediate identification of ideality or transcending with mathematical being, takes philosophy by surprise; philosophy, meanwhile, if it cannot but be wounded, cannot be too surprised either. For there is no philosophy that does not begin by identifying itself like this with a sequence of constituted knowledge that it chooses and that it decides upon. The relation between ontology and mathematics has here merely changed its structure, and is no longer the same as the traditional relation which, dominated by the one-that-is, allowed for a reciprocity of the philosophical and the mathematical. Henceforth (to venture an excessively analogical but nonetheless indicative formulation) the philosophical is that which forecloses mathematics, even while speaking it in the ontology through which it abandons itself to mathematics.

Undulatory void and corpuscular void

The problem is thus not that of making of philosophy this zone of reception and inventory of knowledges and truths—which is what it has always wanted to be anyway—but that of inventing an experimental "chamber" that would receive philosophy so as to transform it. This beginning, by which we assure ourselves as widely as possible of philosophy, consists in including it in a non-philosophical void without which it would be absolute, like Cartesian, psychological, epistemological doubt, finally added together and founded theologically; or absolute like far-eastern nothingness. Logic supposes terms, or a certain ontic content, mathematics being and its empty set, metaphysics theological doubt; but algebra and in particular idempotence imply yet an entirely other type of void. This void imposed by idempotence is no longer definable in ontico-ontological terms or according to a reversible philosophical syntax for which the One and the void, Being and the void are convertible. This void, which is neither that of the One nor that of Being, is that which tolerates radical immanence and must be thought not as simple or correlated term, but instead as undulation and interference. Its essence is undulatory, and no longer corpuscular. Algebra in turn voids the content of terms such as the empty set, but in a broader manner, reserving the rights of a certain indeterminate or under-determined immanence, of a neutralization of corpuscular determinations. Thus disencumbered of its contents, such as nothingness opposed to being, it allows to appear the real of immanence whose form is given by algebra as idempotence.

This radical and generic void is nevertheless articulated, however weakly; there is a *form* of the void, as Badiou and Descartes have recognized—the former in a way perhaps too trenchant and, frankly, corpuscular, the second in a way more acceptable to us and more indeterminate, like the lived. Science neither destroys nor produces its object; it imprints upon it various types of neutralization of double transcendence, a transformation that is its global effect. It does not introduce into the world an absolute void peppered with sparse events. Instead, the philosophical object is flush with the neutral—this is what distinguishes the mathematical voiding of philosophy and its neutralization through quantification. It also describes what there is of the non-vulgar in phenomenology, which, certainly, remains with beings and does not pass over to philosophy as object. Badiou is the Tao of mathematics or the absolute void concluded from mathematics. NP is the radical void obtained through neutralization or under-determination.

With algebra, there are no longer anything but "empty" symbols in this latter, non-formal sense. But it is not these symbols qua void that permit "idempotence" to be thought. What the algebraic void permits is to fill them universally with any content whatsoever of the lived or wave type, of the amplitude type. This is neither the inconsistent multiple nor some other matter like desiring-flux. Neither being nor beings exhaust materiality; idempotence manifests yet another materiality, a more "subjective" materiality, the undulatory lived of which philosophy speaks only allusively, without thematizing it explicitly. Idempotence is univocity itself, its very definition, which is not attached to any being or to Being or to a qualified lived experience (that *becomes* or *undergoes* qua same or univocal). The univocity of the same has a power of speaking itself of ... a power to transit or to conquer; it is *the universal as generic that replaces the all, that is not the all* and that, what is more, can transit it. This power is that of the Mid(-point) [*Mi(-lieu)*], of what we call the strong analytic as weak synthetic, which prepares the immanental under-going.[2] It is thus a void that is not absolute, but radical, via a suspension of its operation. It is the same via resumption, but such that this repetition is suspended. It is thus the same that is indifferent to its operations. And thus, it becomes the principle of superposition. Generic immanence is not a point-One, it is the same-of-the-One. Idempotence is the univocity of thought that is not said in a single sense of every being or of the all, and which must afterward confront the equivocity of the division or partitioning of regions. It is not linked to the One, to the Multiple, to the All. It is messianic univocity for that which is not univocal.

The object-being of philosophy is given by the ultimate laws or laws of the Last Instance that are those of thought, not by laws of the object such as mathematics or even those logics constituted by disciplines in the form of completed-and-closed theories. Here, the laws of thought are those of the lived. They are grasped by algebra, that is to say by logico-mathematics, as necessary, but maximally devoid of all doubly transcendent content. Mathematics and logic together are the laws of transcendent thought; algebra allows us to reduce them without purifying them. The laws of thought act well before the completed theories that serve as substitutes for metaphysical foundations or come to fill them, whereas one must determine laws that are valid for the quantum science of philosophy.

It is not certain that we have a true Idea—this would be dogmatism. We have instead the means, or one principal means, which is mathematics, but precisely a simple means and not a heap of finalities. Dogmatism is mathematics raised to the state of a finality or a measure of all things. We have only an Ariadne's thread to enter into the labyrinth that we ourselves weave from this thread, and it is algebra, not molar logic nor set-theoretical mathematics posited from the outset as a rotating cornerstone that would propel us immediately to the heart of the labyrinth. It is true that we must hold fast to the end of this thread, for the further we progress through the shadows of the labyrinth, the more this thread slips from our hands. Many different doors open, like so many temptations, to the point of revealing to us a prior-to-first unknowing. Logic assures us that there is a thread, its algebraization consigns it to a certain clandestinity; it is made for the subterranean labyrinth of the world and the winding walls of the cosmic, not at all for the open sky of the Greeks. It is this void, a radical void, what we have called a collider that is completed but not closed, that will permit us to enter into the science of the world. It is not a principle or a foundation; we have no ground. The subjects that we are, are mobilized by a void, an unknown attractor. This void may well be that of a generic messianity. This Ariadne's thread allows us to penetrate into the cavern of philosophy without having been in advance dazzled by the sun, and perhaps by philosophy itself.

8

Philo-fiction

Transforming the Parmenidean equation

Philosophy (or at least its transcendental organon) is delimited by Parmenides' axiom-formula. This formula is its minimal kernel—it allows one to know of what one speaks, and to reject from its definition any objectives imposed from outside philosophy (theology, science, art, etc.). Having admitted this kernel (the "Same"), we have discovered that it was susceptible to a variation-transformation of its syntax and semantics. It passes from the Same as reciprocity or auto-reflexivity, to the real One-in-One or to the Same as non-reciprocity, but on condition of exceeding the Parmenidean bloc, and Being in particular. The problem is that of the Real, of its effects upon philosophy when it comes from outside the formula, or more precisely when it under-goes it. NP no longer responds to Parmenides' formula, except in "simplifying" it by including it in immanence. They are "identical-in-the-last-instance," but philosophy is then no longer anything but a material included, in the exteriority of a symptom, in the a priori real. For this to be the case, Being, as Real-One, must not be "separated" from itself by thought, writing, or any other form of alterity. NP is the exposition of a possibility of the last-instance of the canonical formula in the regime of the non-separation of the Real-One, whereas philosophy is its reflected, unique and abusive interpretation—and thus an interpretation divided or repeated from the origin.

NP is the effect of the introduction of a scientific method into Parmenides. In it, the axiom is combined and subordinated to the deployment of a Real that brings its formula to an impasse, exceeding its philosophical auto-reflection. Take Parmenides' formula: by virtue of what do we know that it is philosophical? Doubtless, by virtue of the tradition that has always interpreted it as auto-reflective. We cannot not introduce it, it is already present there; but we can examine its axiom-form, and this in two ways: either classically, by abstracting on the basis of mathematical objects and procedures, whereby we can obtain, at best, the materialist formula that posits Being as identical to a Same that thus divides and subtracts itself from itself. Or we can exit from this formula, on the basis of quantum theory, in the direction of (but beyond) materialism itself. We must *admit that Being is autonomous as One, but also that qua matter it does not separate from itself or subtract itself from itself. We therefore "push" materialism beyond itself* by using the Real or the One-in-One instead of Being, which is thus brought to an impasse. We refuse idealist auto-interpretation, and even what remains of it in the materialism of the formula.

Philosophy is thus placed, not "under mathematical condition," but first of all under real prior-to-priority. The Parmenidean formula, which is auto-interpreted as a foundational axiom of philosophy, is revealed in fact to be but a theorem or a model, and not at all an axiom in the modern sense. For the mathematical axiom-form is distinct from the ancient philosophical (intuitive and ontologico-intellectual) axiom. The latter can be placed under the mathematical occasion, but it is "impossibilized" by the Real that doubtless subtracts it from the mathematics that it under-goes. Here, the Real is not the empty set. But in that case, NP is also no longer a variation on the canonical formula, except as regards its occasional material alone. It is suspended from the Real, and thus *it becomes possible to transform philosophy, Parmenides' formula, into a mere symptom of the Real, and then into the material of philo-fiction, and moreover into a model of philo-fiction.* This is a new form for philosophy, which has had others, all deriving from the primacy of thought if not that of consciousness (even in Marx, it does not find a truly new form, having only the thesis-form, which Marx proposed as the basis of historico-economic determinations). All the same, we understand that it is not a matter of imposing on the Logos, which would not tolerate it, any basis whatever from outside; philosophy must be able, qua philosophy, to become meta-language, symptom and model and, in doing so, to become immanent or simply a priori Logos. Philosophy remains at least a norm for the materiality of discourse, but it is also preposed as symptom and material. The radical is on the edge of the Logos, but as *its* edge; it is the

Logos reduced to the state of the edge of the Real. This is the distinction between marginality and messianity. Philo-fiction is this edge of the Real that accompanies it without speaking it, as non-Logos or Verb of the generic subject.

Against the mathematical contemplation of philosophy

It cannot be said that knowledge that is generic or (in its own way) gnostic is a unitary science, fully delimited, in the classical sense, by a domain of objects and a theory. It is a multiplicity (if not a coalition) of scientific knowledges, not a theory axiomatically closed onto itself by a principle of identity. There is *some* mathematics, some logic, some topology, various fragments of science—not one single science with a completed domain that would fall back on its object, philosophy, from within or without, but one unique lived wave function or state vector, making these knowledges interfere *with* philosophy. A science of philosophy must superpose many scientific instances, using, for example, algebra and logic or the laws of pure thought. And only quantum theory, which has a certain vocation to be an epistemology of philosophy, can effectuate these laws (the prior-to-first ante-placement or ante-version, idempotence, unilaterality, unifaciality or unilateral complementarity). To act upon philosophy, rather than to contemplate it one more time—this is our imperative, and quantum theory is of the order of the means of man as Last Instance; it is not the mirror in which philosophy admires itself again and always. It is not philosophy that must be sterile—it always has been, in its own way, a way other than that of the unconscious that knows no (philosophical) contradiction (Freud). Certain recent attempts, including Badiou's, have reached the limit of ascetic saturation, exclusively mathematicizing at the risk of no longer being capable of the experimental practice of their object that quantum theory retains. The unconscious might, for example, content itself with combinatory mathematics and topology (Lacan), at the risk of giving rise to a formal and contemplative psychoanalysis that connects, in uncertain manner, a formalism to an empiricism of the imaginary; or else a mathematicizing materialism as simple identity between a formal philosophy and a sufficient and "demonstrative" mathematics. But the science of philosophy necessitates (given the complexity of its object) that the pilot-science should be quantum theory—physics, rather than mathematics alone. A conceptual formalism, as abstract as it may be, conducts the experimental work on its object. The inconsistent multiple gives way to a molar materialism of the void, a subtle form of conceptual atomism that destroys the superposition of knowledges and reestablishes the old Platonic style of philosophy—as if humans, the beings who practice the middle way [*la voie du mi(-lieu)*] and its indiscernible paths, had to practice it as a space strung between two molar limits, between divine or superhuman inspiration and the body of mathematics, one being unbreathable, the other breathtaking, in both cases because one sought to impose them as necessary and sufficient trajectories of existence. To liberate ourselves from the Platonic hypothecation of philosophy to mathematics, which makes philosophy closed to the non-mathematician, let us try another hypothesis: the quantum theory of the lived that is simply foreclosed to the philosopher.

From the philosophical tale
to the science of philosophy

Science is foreclosed to philosophy, let us accept this hypothesis— but foreclosed unilaterally and for itself alone. Because, in contrast, philosophy is sutured to science. We make the *apparently* inverse hypothesis to Badiou's, for whom philosophy must not be sutured to science. We dualyze the concept of suture: philosophy is a unilateral complement to science, and it will be used as a hermeneutic at the service of the latter. It thus redis-covers a materiality and a utility that withdraw it into a proud, stellar solitude. For what could philosophy be good for, apart from affirming that one is a philosopher; this we know already by hearsay, it is an act of self-affirmation. Philosophy is a sponta-neity that is practiced and that proclaims itself without knowing itself (like gnosis—but philosophy is an anti-gnosis or a gnosis of transcendence).

What would it mean to de-suture science and philosophy? To de-suture poem and philosophy? Certainly not to lead philosophy into "disaster" (Badiou), but simply to conserve a relative autonomy for it. But there is too much equivocity in this formula. Either this formula of de-suturation understood in the absolute signifies a planification of corpuscular instances, their separation through a bilateral gesture dedicated to the absolute, that re-introduces, on the sly, the specular relations concealed in the absolute, so that apparently there is no longer any place for a suture or a minimum of relation. At best one admits that there subsists a suture between opposites, but then it is essentially philosophical, and depends upon a background materialist position, and thus on a science understood classically as objectivation. Or else we embark upon a new adventure, a paradoxical combination, that of the (non numerical-quantitative) "quantification" of philosophy. A "quantification" which, without believing that it destroys every suture or gives a still-philosophical materialist version of it, is content to unilateralize it. As an adjoint quantification of instances-phases, it is materiel but not materialist, and is still not understood necessarily as objectivating. Radical unilateralization transforms simultaneously materiality (preventing it from turning into materialism) and the suture (preventing it from turning into bilateral or absolute relation). There will always be a certain relation, but a "simplified" one. At one end or "side" (but one that remains virtual) it is a non-relation, One via radical immanence; and on the "other" side, a semi-relation, that is to say a "contribution" (unilation) that exists the former as front, the true and only side possible.

This contribution can then be grasped in twofold manner: as lived, on the side of the science-subject, who is not especially objectivation, and as perceived, from the point of view of the contribution itself, as duality of a relation. The contribution is

in itself conveyed by immanence or superposition, and is thus
unilateral as act. But what is contributed, causes this act to be
seen as bilateral—the philosophical appearance of the in-itself.
Unilateral duality—this is what is proper to non-philosophy;
but not without the context of the generic, that is to say, a
certain quantum resumption via superposition. It is obviously
a cutting weapon, but one that is less weightless than dialectics;
a duality that "forces" all metaphysical dualities or amphibolies,
such as that of form/matter, and in particular positions of the
Multiple and the One—all ternary or triadic syntaxes such as the
transcendental, on whose basis philosophical assemblages can
be composed. As soon as there is a positing of philosophy taken
as self-evident, then the rupture supposedly operated by the
generic procedures can never be consummated. To oppose the
matheme to the poem does not truly affect philosophy, or has
few effects upon it—effects that remain marginal or positional
(sheltering the materialist who would remain a philosopher).
The old mythological narrative persists in the form of the Very
Grand Narrative of the materialist whose announced rupture
with the poem as determining condition is not consummated.
The absolute or spontaneous materialist position is so uncertain
of itself that it needs to repeat itself, the repetition of "manifestos"
in the modern manner. To these forms of doubt and thus
of dogmatic proposition and compensatory re-affirmation, we
shall oppose the frank decision of the wager and of invention,
the resumption of immanence, so as to relieve ourselves of
spontaneous self-belief and philosophical narcissism.

For example, philosophers are obliged to treat philosophy as an object in itself, but they go no further, and continue to opt arbitrarily for one or another variant of idealism or materialism. They thus proceed cynically, without going to the end of the reduction of their presupposition. Non-philosophy also presupposes the in-itself, but complicates it, for at the same time it treats it as a symptom under radical immanence or "under (quantum) science," as objective appearance—which enables it to escape the naive materialist position. Badiou must treat mathematical objectivity as an equivalent form of symptom, but this time "under philosophy." His meta-ontology does not escape the philosophical position of materialism, and the presupposition is not at all the same. For the philosopher, philosophy is an object in itself, an object he does not examine qua symptom of the scientific type or qua deprived of its materialist positing, but at best as a philosophical given. This is why, *insofar as he does not really pass into philosophy deployed as scientific symptom, he simply tells a philosophical tale about a positive science*—he repeats the mythological style, whereas the Greek physiologists (rather than Plato) inaugurated a scientific vision of the object "philosophy."

Non-standard epistemology, rather than the auto-modelization of epistemology

We must seek very deeply, in the most intimate mechanism of epistemology, the monotony of the criteria that it intends to affix to science. Philosophy and epistemology are simple, bi-univocal relations, with a certain twist, between a philosophy and a science. Merely posing the problem obliges us to imagine that one unique epistemology exists in principle, and is varied only by systems and disciplines, that is to say externally and contingently. Another consequence is that this mono-epistemology posits the unicity of the relation: it defines what a philosophy is, but above all, what a science is. It is a discipline now descriptive of scientific practice, now normative, setting the criteria of the scientific and thus of that which is least or not at all scientific; and then, ultimately, it becomes a foundational discipline as soon as it can. Philosophy, above all that of Platonic inspiration, is auto-modelizing and thus unique in principle; but at the same time, it obliges science, a determined science, and not only mechanics, also to be auto-normative. The auto-modelization of philosophy postulates the auto-modelization of a determined science, and of science in general, for itself. And this is the origin of epistemological stereotypes and of their lack of inventiveness. The new problem is as follows: *how to render epistemology and the philosophy of sciences themselves inventive, how to have done with auto-epistemology.*

Non-standard philosophy is thus made to struggle against this classical or auto-modelizing epistemology. It is never an example for itself, but finds its models elsewhere, so that a determinate epistemology cannot be an example for another but, at the most, a model for another. To achieve this, we must renounce the traditional confrontation of two in-itselfs (a confrontation Badiou still partially stages), of a determinate science and a determinate philosophical position, in this case materialism. It is possible to posit an immanent fusion or super-position of a science and an ontology, a fusion that avoids a dispersion of knowledges or a multiplication of cuts (Foucault) just as it avoids an authoritarian planification. Now, Badiou realizes the need to combat epistemological power, to "fuse" the Set and Being from the outset. But he does not go to the end of the operation of the destruction of the Principle of Sufficient Philosophy. He keeps in reserve the materialist position, which remains there, overlooking everything, in waiting to take control of the procedure philosophically. As to the all of philosophy, it is converted into a function of reception and compossibility. We cannot content ourselves with cutting into the all of philosophy, fusing a part of it with mathematics, and preserving another material part as a control agency. The fusion must be carried out on the *whole* of the materiality of philosophy, leaving out of this fusion only its formal sufficiency, which is "our" concept of the "representation" that philosophers like to criticize. Badiou does indeed borrow this matrix, which we also call "generic," but he interprets it with philosophy as function and as dominant, whereas we interpret it with a science, quantum theory, as generic factor of immanence, which permits us to no longer have to make a choice within philosophy. In other words, he superimposes upon the fusion philosophical Decision, whose authority he conserves, and which divides philosophy into two parts, whereas we under-determine the fusion though quantum thought, and *separate without division* the material all of philosophy, and its supposedly sufficient status. Decisionism, like activism, is a constant of the philosophical tradition, and of primers of the gesture of generalized deconstruction (Derrida). They go hand-in-hand with the ideal of the unity of the philosophical all, and reproduce the latter. We understand that, with such mechanisms, it is impossible to go to the end of philosophical sufficiency, which is thus condemned to be reproduced once again.

From materialism to philo-fiction

It is true that philosophy does not produce truths; there is something sterile about it, a sterility either by excess (but then one would have to create a replacement meta-ontology that knew and spoke truth) or by default and transcendental illusion (but it is NP that does this work of the "non-" truth—which is not truth's contrary as absolute non-truth). Materialism works with a precise, local science, interpreting and contemplating it, but does not transform it, any more than idealism does, and still less their epistemological complex; it contemplates truths produced elsewhere. Mathematicizing materialism is a division of labor. Its two sides would have to have come from the same Last Instance, and not have formed a hierarchy or a duality inside of a torsion or a duplicity, thus inside a still-imaginary All. In any case, what is called for is an organization founded on a "without-relation" even in the relations that we give ourselves as material. The Real is this true without-relation, but one that under-goes the relation that it contributes. Materialism gives itself this "without-relation" in the form of the identity of mathematics and Being (withdrawn from philosophy), an enigmatic and flattened identity accompanied by meta-ontology, the remainder of philosophy. In OV, mathematics is the materialist base supposed by a meta-ontology still in the grip of philosophy, so that the cooperation of Being is required to give it a hand. In NP, the Real-One is a base already in the grip of philosophy, but we require a work of under-going and thus of superposition, with a subtractive effect of the a priori, to establish good order and to reduce philosophy to the state of philo-fiction. In materialism, one needs a philosophical decision to separate itself as ontology—a decision that needs to be justified or founded externally by mathematics. Thought is requisitioned as Being and meta-ontology, a thought in excess over mathematics; and is then rejected and doubled as philosophy. The philosophical All, doubtless imaginary, amputates itself from Being and from ontology, and at the same time is rejected as a philosophical margin. For NP, the All of philosophy is not shared-out/partitioned, but reduced without division, so that it is identity by superposition of the Real and of the Logos determined as a priori, *and* in-the-last-instance unilateral margin. From our point of view, materialism (not to mention idealism) is made possible by an insufficient analysis of philosophical duplicity. Spontaneous philosophism believes in the simplicity of the philosophical gesture and moves within it, refusing to realize that it is already encompassed by the philosophical decision that anticipates itself.

NP is a scenario of the future as that which under-goes. The scenario is the emergence of the unilateral a priori, of a space or a base whose law is unilaterality. It is the quarter-scene, where the circle of representation is flattened and has only one side. We must de-theatricalize the scenarios of the imagination. It is not a matter of a foundation of possible scenarios, but of the real scenario fabricated in the under-going, that real scenario of which all philosophical scenarios are but models. Philosophy is fundamentally a theatre that denies itself as such, that cannot recognize itself as final duplicity, as a tragedy and a comedy of self-repetition. A *deus ex machina*: the philosopher seems to disappear into philosophy, but in reality projects himself specularly, like a curious god contemplating this game. Materialism begins to simplify the theatre: the philosopher is still necessary—no longer as a god, but in the wings, where he hides himself so as to pull the strings of matter and thought, of Being and consciousness. In materialism, the double or duplicitous philosopher still partitions himself out into two roles; or divides himself (rather than dualysing himself). He is a determinate thought that receives truths without being able to create them, but he is also this meta-ontologue of mathematical Being, this weakened philosopher at the service of mathematical matter, who helps to produce truths.

From idealist materialism to NP, we pass from philosophy as a still somewhat determining thought-without-truth of Truth, to philo-fiction, which is no longer determining at all, or only qua symptom. Philo-fiction is a supplementary freeing of the Logos, even if a last link of virtuality between Real and Logos is inscribed in the latter, that is to say, in the material or the symptom. Philosophy is freed from its subjection to the Real at the extreme possible limit, where the only residual link is occasional. Materialism unbinds matter, but also thought or the autonomy of philosophy, or else enchains a half of itself; but NP frees it as a fiction, which no longer has anything but one last link with philosophical sufficiency. Delivering it from the substantial or humanist burdens of the Real, it negates only that part of it that can be negated—its sufficiency; it lightens philosophy in preparation for its radical under-going.

Philosophy as model of philo-fiction

That the Real should not be first, that is to say not counted or named as One, Two or Three (the Three of philosophy), is an important trait that brings the Real close to Being as multiple of multiples. But it is no longer decisive in this context, which is no longer numerical or even quantitative, and which intends not to measure the Real with coupled attributes (which are mere variables, even if they are obtained by subtraction) but to posit a unilateral complementarity for all couplets of properties.

A capital feature of NP is the substitution of the modelization, through philosophy, of the radically immanent Real, for the philosophical reduction or interpretation of the latter. Philosophy is spontaneously a reduction of the Real and thus its division; it intends to transform it within certain limits but in NP it loses this constitutive and destructive function, and acquires another function, that of the simple modelization of the Real and of philo-fiction. It is philosophical sufficiency that is reduced, not the Real. NP thus implies an inversion between the Real and philosophy: the latter ceases to be the object of the former, the former ceases to be the subject that decides the latter. In this way, modelization replaces reduction, withdrawal and subtraction, all of which are still philosophical operations. We must accept that philosophy changes its function globally, not just its form or its modality; that it is in reality a modelization of another thought, philo-fiction. To formalize philosophy, it is necessary to submit it to the Real, to make of philo-fiction the science of the Real. Whence a new conception of the Real, extricated from philosophy and science alike; must we invoke the religious to formulate such a conception? Our problem is not that of whether to follow religion or science or philosophy, but that of treating philosophy, and thus also its religious extremity, as a modelization of the Real; that of inventing a philo-fictional formalism of which science, philosophy and religion will be modelizations. The problem is no longer that of the death or the end of philosophy, of its gathering into itself, of its repetition or its recommencement. The project is less than this, but at the same time more ambitious: the problem is of that of its global mutation, of the loss of its sufficiency, that of finding a philo-fictional, and religious-fictional (and also science-fictional) formalism that explains these phenomena. We abandon the old usage of thought, always referred back to itself; it passes a threshold of materiality and of formalism. The obsession with the death of philosophy has given way to that of its sufficiency, which includes its excess and its decline. In consequence, we have to renounce the characteristic, celebrated and foundational gestures, which will henceforth be but local means (founding, reducing, subtracting, withdrawing, suspecting, critiquing, anticipating/retarding, overthrowing, meditating, elucidating, analyzing, synthetizing, deconstructing and constructing, etc.). Obviously this is, in a sense, to justify wholly the philosophical act in its material effectivity, to pronounce not its death but its transformation, and simultaneously its constitution as a model.

We eliminate the theoreticist Real qua Greek contracted and divine self-contemplation, which supposes an external philosophy using its authority and the PSP, and which does not achieve immanence, but conserves the religious background. *A fortiori* Badiou is a great director and manipulator of knowledges. It will be a matter (again, otherwise) of knowing if one philosophizes with Saint Paul—an authoritarian and a volunteer keen to become the Master of Christians (or, respectively, of the philosophical Church) or if one philosophizes with Christ; with the copy or with the original, we might say, in Platonic terms that are not quite apt here; with the apostle or with the Christ? Despite the immanence of contemplation, or self-contemplation, there is a doubling between the philosopher and the soul. Precisely, on one hand, a specular doubling between auto-contracted or intellectual identity, and on the other a philosopher *ex machina*. Whereas in NP, there is a unilateral duality between generic Man and the subject who assumes philosophical labor.

Non-Marxism or "non-standard Marxism"

We can become obsessed with Marxist man and the Marxist subject, but there is no point in obsessing about the term

"Marxism," which must be conserved because Marx is inseparable from the complex, multiple, symptomatic tradition to which he gave birth, and because the term Marxism is fortunately generic, unlike "Marxian," which reflects a transcendental ego (Henry and others) or an individual, the supposed individual Marx. It is indeed the term "Marxism" that must be complexified through science, so as to extricate it from philosophical antinomies and their harassing "universality."

OV and NP both seek a form of Marx's Revolutionary Science, a form that would be at once theoretically acceptable, and most able to realize certain of the promises of the latter. For us, the heart of Marxism lies in a new science, for which philosophy is *also* required. Its global scientific model is mechanics, with algebraic and Darwinian fringes; its philosophical model is a certain overturning of Hegel; its object is history and societies in history. One might imagine that there is an apparent partitioning between the scientific aspect (Historical Materialism—HM) that NP assumes, and the philosophical aspect (Dialectical Materialism—DM) that OV assumes, and transforms into Materialist Dialectic (MD). Whilst not exactly false, this distinction is perhaps too simple. Because philosophy intervenes in NP or in generic science; and because science is invested in the Materialist Dialectic, but under a philosophical reversal. Materialism arrives as an empty position of principle without concrete materiality, as if mathematics did not penetrate matter, and remained in its self-contemplation in the mirror of philosophy. Despite this, there is indeed a tendency for OV to proceed through DM inverted into MD, and for NP to operate instead through HM. HM is profoundly transformed in NP; DM is simply rejected, abandoned because of the dialectic (the latter is replaced by unilaterality, which is not a sub-dialectic despite its duality), and because its materialism is replaced by materiality (which is not a watered-down materialist thesis). From HM we retain (transformed within NP) science, the Last Instance, the "generic" comprehension of history as world and capital, the fusion of theory and the masses (not the fusion of mathematics and ontology but that of quantum theory and the lived of the subject); and finally, the duality of infrastructure and superstructure, in the form of the wave/particle *model*. It is a transformation of Marxism through the contribution of quantum theory, or again, Marxism put under condition of quantum theory, rather than that of Hegel's philosophical science (whether overturned or not).

Let us try to interpret the duel structure of these post-Marxisms, through the generic matrix that serves as our guide. Firstly, OV or MD: D and M are possible variables, whose fusion or product is made either under M, or under D—that is, under materialism (matter) or under dialectic (philosophy). But these two solutions come to almost the same thing, for matter is here materialism—still a philosophy. The maximal withdrawal or distancing of science that Badiou carries out, on the basis of the maximal place of science, is not at all a weakening of philosophical sufficiency (which retains, on the contrary, its entitlement to glory, being voided only of its concrete substance) any more than it is a reinforcement of science, which still labors under that distant imperial domination. We might even ask whether the unity of science would not be cut in two with this planified return or reversal that maintains the primacy of philosophy.

The formula M+D under M might signify, strictly speaking, a superposition of matter or of the science of matter with itself—which would not be a philosophical doubling or a repetition, but a quantum or undulatory operation. Read in this way, the duel formula of Marxism signifies a "requantification" of materiality, but without the materialist thesis that is a dialectical effect or doubling; an idealization that is philosophical, not scientific. A unified theory of science and of philosophy must be realized in the conjoint modes of scientific discovery and philosophical invention.

As for NP, two conditions, not just one, are necessary in order to obtain a truly unified theory of science and philosophy or a "generic science" (another, more precise name for NP): (1) To posit the primacy of the prior-to-priority of immanence via superposition, or to do more than invert philosophical duality. (2) To fulfill and assure this prior-to-priority of immanence through the schema of the imaginary or complex number. All alone this schema yields quantum physics, which is a positive science in a relation of reciprocal exteriority with philosophy. These two operations permit the effectuation of the science of an object that always holds, directly or indirectly, to philosophy as material or symptom without sufficiency. This is why NP as science of philosophy is the greatest amplitude of thought, capable of transforming these disciplines. These operations together introduce a concept of the complex or implicated function into the variables, like the complex numbers used in quantum theory. To transform the old ideal of the foundation into a bound variable or into a generic constant of knowledges whose vectors are superposed, is to vanquish philosophy, but also the eclecticism that lurks in its mélanges and that comes out in its practices.

It is also to extract the Marxist kernel from philosophy, and not only from idealist dialectics; to understand that Marxism is oriented by the Idea of a generically unified theory of science and philosophy. Its structuralist interpretation was a first step toward this type of solution, but it is possible to interpret it as a lived via superposition—not as ego or organic transcendental force (Michel Henry) but as organic immanental force. If we interpret quantum theory as the condition for obtaining a Last Instance, it is possible, inversely, to understand the material basis of HM as superposition, but also the impotence of ideology to represent the Last Instance as a logic of superposed forces. To extract Marx from mechanism and conceptual atomism, and this without passing through a transcendental subject, but instead through an immanental instance adding together science and philosophy—this is what is at stake. The science of history is not obtained through a coalition or synthesis of the "bourgeois" science of history and a materialist philosophy inherited from Hegel, but through their *quantum superposition*. It is necessary to oppose this generic displacement/inversion on the terrain of immanence to the Feuerbachian genericity that inverts the terms, but transcendently, without giving a primacy to immanence—a necessary condition in order to obtain generic superposition.

Marxism and psychoanalysis, moreover, function according to a certain usage or a certain interpretation of the principle of superposition, but are inverted epistemologies of them, on the way to unilateralization, operating under the guidance of science, or even of a coalition of sciences, as psychoanalysis has demonstrated and as Marxism has attempted, in the form polemically called "imaginary," coalescing politics, economics, philosophy— remaking a mélange in transcendence for a "science of history" and "of society" to which it would at the same time limit HM. Marx is returned to the mélanges, in the absence of any real means corresponding to his concept—the badly named (that is to say named in bourgeois fashion) HM—materialism being the reversal of the Hegelian Idea, and history being the limited object that occupies the place of philosophy. Equally, psychoanalysis can hardly extract itself from the infantile mélanges of physical, biological, mathematical, cultural sciences, "imaginary" or just "infantile psychoanalyses." Because they have given rise to formations that are still transcendent, Marx and Freud await their immanent transformation that will allow the introduction of a real scientific advance, like quantum theory, in these disciplines. They announce the transformation of these disciplines—a non-hermeneutic transformation, contrary to Foucault's interpretation. Foucault's residual hermeneuticism corresponds to an imaginary-objective science, insofar as immanence has not, ultimately, been thought; and to think immanence is firstly to put it, as superposition, in the position of an ultimation that is first or of the Last Instance.

These sciences that tend toward the generic refusal to make of man a Greek foundation, so as to make of him the function of an immanent knowledge, represent a certain gnostic tradition that it becomes possible to reevaluate, and in which it would be more interesting to include them than in Hegelian philosophy or (even more sadly) in a reflexive tradition. Neither Freud nor Marx lacked adversaries that abominated in them the spirit of gnosis and of a certain heresy. Why not see in them, pushing the spirit of perspectivist interpretations as far as possible, "Jewish histories," if this fits; or even "Jewish heresies," so as to put a final point on the hesitations and attain the point of provocation on whose basis the Adversary is discovered (in defense, one distinguishes a priori between the point of indignation and the point of provocation). Obviously, this fragmented tradition of gnostic knowledge as non-eclectic integration of knowledges is confirmed and re-utilized after the fact by the quantum-generic spirit rather than by a too-unitary mechanism. The first ultimation comes down, in this broadened interpretation of gnosis, to positing *gnosis* as knowledge of-the-last-instance, a knowledge that defines man as a prior-to-priority that will never be a foundation or a beginning, except in the Greek appearance of priority and fundamentality. NP is a function of the addition of a scientific discovery, here resumed, and a philosophical invention. Without foundations, without theses even, non-philosophy has only, and still, "principles."

The non-act and its action; under and over-potentialization

We have already distinguished the non-act from immanence and its proper action. We must give a little more detail, and not confuse the radical or immanent Real with the supposedly absolute Real, as a substantial or spiritual thing for example. Their modes of action are extremely different, like an under-potentialization and an over-potentialization. The radical Real is "impossible" as soon as put into unilateral complementarity with the possible. Radical rather than absolute, it has no relation or interface, no common face that it would idealize and conserve with the world or with the symbolic; it has only a uniface "with" the world or drawn *occasionally* from the world. The symbolic would seize the Real that cannot seize it reciprocally, that can neither act nor react in the mechanical and reciprocal sense. There is no solution other than to subtract from the double transcendence of the symbolic (and of mathematics) a now simple transcending, to "attract" or to "draw" to it the corpuscle so as to make of it a particle, in the sole mode of unilateral transfer that the symbolic did not expect; to render it immanent in turn, but only on one face or one "side" of itself. Nothing of the symbolic can be rendered immanent except that which the Real tolerates in virtue of its immanence of superposition. Head-on capture is excluded, as is flight, exteriorization along with retreat; its being is the prior-to-first superposition. The Real is not at all that of transcendence as doublet, neither exvagination nor invagination, neither convexity nor concavity. Nonetheless, as Last Instance, it affects the symbolic, itself become in-immanence according to its own mode. Here is the process of quasi-transfer that we sought, instead of the instance of the Other, to explain that the Real in its essence as superposition should be a non-acting capable of "acting" non-mechanically in the form of a simple under-potentialization or under-determination of transcendence. The superposition proper to immanence is the final "positivity" that can explain the effect of subtraction from simple, noematic or particulate transcendence, from the transcendence that from the outset is always in doublet. Badiou explains subtraction via the void, that is to say in an *absolutely* passive manner, whereas NP explains it as a *radically* passive (that is to say, non-contemplative) effect, generated or resumed by an occasional cause or a unilateral complementarity. Badiou holds to a contemplative materialism, as Marx would say, even while being obliged to suppose that it has an abstract or quasi-transcendental operativity flattened onto it. This is again the risk of an intermediary instance or a mediation, this time necessitated by the mathematical void which itself is too inert, and which thus has need of a transcendent but hidden organon. The choice is between a mathematicism that is spontaneously consonant with the materialist void, and a physics of superposition that, from the outset, makes of real immanence as last instance a minimal practical human organon. *The means or the mediation adds nothing real to the Real that is continued in it, only to the reality that takes place as occasional. The generic Subject as Last Instance is immediately an immanent force of means—this is what we call the mediate-without-mediation or the mediatum.*

Now, on the side of reduced transcendence, if one supposes it isolated from its pulsion, reality is added to the Real (but "under" the Real)—a sterile addition with regard to the Real, just as idempotence would have it, but one that unleashes the particulate becoming. From this angle, the Real that includes and configures the particle, and which itself is unifacial, seems this time to act as a bifacial Other-than... acting precisely upon the world, like a new instance of radical alterity (not absolute alterity, as, for example, in Levinas). The under-potentialization to which the non-act leads is manifested in the least-act that it then exerts as Other-than or Stranger-subject upon the double transcendence of the world that it simplifies. It is manifested on first appearance as an acting of the world upon the world, but one affected by an alterity that philosophers confuse with under-potentialization—whereas this phenomenon is but a modelization of the least-act by worldy acting. Qua a priori, the particle is the manifestation of the suspended world, of halted sufficiency, and is found charged with the tasks of the a priori, those of the transformation of the philo-world into philo-fiction. Immanent non-acting underdetermines the weak act or the least-act of that transformation which is the only possibility left to man.

If philosophy brings together all aspects of the possible, the radical Real via superposition cannot, inversely, be possibilized by logic or philosophy, to which it is foreclosed. It is rather that this Real impossibilizes them, transforms them by under-determining them through the a priori of the Impossible. To be subtracted, itself, from the particulate a priori (non-commutativity) is the essence of the sole cause (the Last Instance or the generic Subject) that can act through its non-acting. But there subsists a "bond" of a priori unilaterality between generic Man and the world qua occasional; this unilateral link is the equivalent of "being-for" the world, it is their unilateral complementarity.

Qua separated, and because it is separated, the generic Subject is nevertheless destined a priori for the world, but this is not a *com*-portment, it is the real possibility-(of)-impossibility, a contribution of the world rather than a com-portment with it. The Real "contributes" the world by impossibilizing it as world but leaving it as world.

The Real, thanks to the Other-than... in the figure of which it announces itself to the world, and that it is, insofar as occasionally it can speak itself (a speaking whose claims it has already suspended) can act, finally, upon the possible, without being its opposite, without acting directly upon it, but by suspending its sufficiency. The Real as a priori is impossible-for ... logical contradiction, but it is in this way that it gives or makes visible originarily (that is to say, transforms) logical contradiction, and all those principles that Aristotle charged philosophy and the real with, as Being and Thought. Alongside the truths of fact and the logical truths that are the funds of philosophical commerce, transforming them by "impossibilizing" them, the Real manifests necessary and impossible truths, truths whose impossibility is necessary. The Real is impossible when it acts as Other-than particulate or a priori; it is *the a priori of impossibility* necessary to under-determine or to transform the given world or the possible world, suspending the sufficiency of logical possibility, illegalizing legality without destroying it, putting into effect everywhere an impossibilization of functionings without annihilating them. The Real of immanence, by virtue of the particle that it configures, is the non-dialectical solution to contradiction and to antinomies.

It impossibilizes logic and theory without destroying them, instead simplifying them into their materiality, reducing them to the state of fiction—but a logic-fiction or philo-fiction. It gives to deployed theory, to all of fictional materiality, its force of "formalism," for which reality, the empirical, and ideality are all *of* fictional materiality, but without constitutive effect *upon* it.

From metaphor to unilateral complementarity

To admit this mutation, which imposes upon philosophy a physical rather than a linguistic model, to dissociate thinking and logos, we must admit that the physical level does not annul the linguistic surface of philosophy, but that its quantum (undulatory and particulate) materiality and its quantware syntax (rather than logical syntax) are immanent to this linguistic surface, and imply its quantum treatment or transform it. Just as the most mathematical physics also speaks in natural and common language (albeit not unproblematically), so the quantum theory of philosophy is spoken in natural language—a situation rather more convenient than that of physics, since the two have a natural language in common. We must reconsider the status of metaphor, and avoid saying, as Deleuze does, that there is no such thing; we must take up this problem, which is that of the confrontation of mathematical language and the natural language of life in the world. The solution consists in treating natural language itself as a meta-language of that quantum theory of philosophy, and as being also a phenomenon intelligible in quantum-theoretical terms—that is to say, a particulate phenomenon. And on the other hand, for its part, the quantum physics required here must be transformed by natural language, through its translation into a quantum or quantial thought, as the generic matrix demands. In order to do so, must we invoke the indirect language of quantum physicists, and the whole problem of the natural interpretation of quantum theory? Why would the world be a metaphor of mathematics, except, perhaps, from their point of view—and in any case, Gödel prohibits this absolutizing of mathematics. It itself has need of a natural meta-language, and thus the situation of a double tension is unavoidable. Unilateral duality precisely can resolve this problem in the form of a unilateral complementarity of quantum theory and meta-language, which is the true Bohr complementarity of mathematics (algebra) and language, not just that of wave and particle. We must extend and transform Bohr's special complementarity in the direction of a more general complementarity of the micro- and macroscopic, applied to philosophy and quantum theory together. Is not this generic complementarity the real content of what we call metaphor in the case of philosophy, and indirect language in the case of science? Is it not a means to resolve the question of indirect languages? We must pursue as far as possible a "quantification" of natural and philosophical language, so as to be able to deduce the latter as particulate. General complementarity as a product of extremes, but resumed generically, is perhaps the solution that was there from the start, and was not therefore dependent on philosophy and quantum theory as disciplines in exteriority one in relation to the other. The problem is from the outset regulated in-the-last-instance as, already, providing its own solution: there is not philosophy on one side and quantum theory on the other, each delivered to the PSP and PSM that signify their reciprocal exteriority, that is to say their sufficiency. We have posited a priori the conditions for the disciplines no longer being sufficient except in appearance, and for their admitting their generic or inverse (but precisely not equal) translations from the outset. This is to treat already according to Heisenberg's Uncertainty Principle the problem of translations, which, moreover, do not reform a reciprocal interiority, any more than an exteriority, no more a substance than an atomism. It is precisely the *radical* indetermination in principle of these translations (not entirely in Quine's sense) that the unilateral complementarity of mathematics and philosophy registers. Moreover, mathematics itself is translated philosophically once the product is inscribed in parentheses—this is the phenomenon we call the rational quantum kernel, or quantware. Quantware comes in the form of the philosophical translation of quantum theory; it constitutes, already, a denumerization and a deconceptualization that prepare their unilateral complementarity. Unilateral duality has no sense except in the parentheses of inverse products, and thus as non-readable, non-decipherable philosophically, and, equally, non-readable in purely quantum-theoretical manner. Unilateral duality is a quantware concept, not a software concept. To interpret it, we must use concepts and quantum theory in a relation of wave-particle correlation, thus in the generic form of complementarity.

The entire elaboration of the generic matrix is such an operation of complementarity, or resolution of metaphor.

It is not that metaphor does not exist; but it certainly does not regulate the problem sufficiently. In the same way, the quantification of concepts is not sufficient quantum theory, but its use as a means. Thus, in the generic complementarity assured by radical immanence, everything that is used is used as means and not as sufficient finality. This is what settles the question of metaphor, in the sense that the excess of meta-phor is that of a transcendence that doubles itself, and that unilateral complementarity makes the correlation of dialectical opposites redescend to the plane of generic immanence; the Real under-determines or under-potentializes metaphor. Our generic matrix is an experimental chamber of the transformation of knowledges and of their philosophical relations as metaphors. It is truly the fusion of quantum theory and philosophy, whose unity in the form of their inverted products is under-determined by quantum theory, no longer positive or mathematicized, but already philosophized, or at least reduced, by generic complementarity. We must treat metaphor generically, and not leave it either to internal relations or external relations; the correlation, or rather unilation, of unilateral complementarity is neither substantial nor atomic.

In what sense is the stranger "undocumented"?[1] Toward a generic ethics of philosophy

We have treated generically, not philosophically, the philosopher-Adversary, discussed his method of thinking without negating its materiality, but only its PSP and its PSM, the two pillars of his formal and authoritarian sufficiency. We now no longer work under a thesis, axiom or principle, within a discursivity, but in an experimental matrix—strictly speaking, under variables and parameters, in conformity with the ethics of means. Under condition of their withdrawal, we can always consider those remnants, philosophy's hypotheses and theses of every sort, as variables conjugated but under-determined by the generic hypothesis of radicality or of the One-in-One obtained via superposition. We can make ourselves an "idea" of non-philosophy as ethics of philosophy put under condition of humans understood not as individual subjects, but as generic subjects who only possess an individual subject qua margin of transcendence.

We can transform another of Badiou's guiding threads into an Ariadne's thread to explore our matrix: philosophers willingly put forward the hypothesis of an *absolute* or *hyperbolic* poverty. Badiou does so too, with the figure of the undocumented Stranger, who is a sort of Archimedean point, a figure or concentrate of his philosophy, and also a margin of contemporary philosophy. This Stranger is stripped of everything, but not of the hope of obtaining, all the same, the documents to authorize his residency; hope as the last predicate still equivalent to the All, or outlining its image. The Stranger is an absolute limit, a limit capable of reversing itself dialectically into its opposite, as is the rule with the idealism of modern philosophers, a rule of All to All. For philosophical hypotheses are made to reverse into their opposite, whether the Idea of communism or the Reign of ends. Even Lacan, as Derrida has shown, and Badiou, as we have tried to do, do not escape the pointillized All, the transparency or the mirror that accompanies the typically philosophical little ruse of the famous "not-all." The philosophical individual is always all-document, whether he has documents or not—to think otherwise would be to abusively limit the problem, like philosophers who intra-philosophically partition their object. Absolute poverty allows a reversal, for example, of nihilism into counter-nihilism; it is the form of Cartesian or absolute doubt that the proletariat deprived of "all" in Marx's sense (denuded of all predicates but perhaps not yet of All) can also assume. What is ultimately proper to the philosopher is to be denuded of all, to the point of his death, *except* his death, inclusive of which he cannot undo or be undone. Even Badiou's materialism, which leads his specular image from torsion to torsion, cannot disburden him of it. Philosophy is not the scientific or generic test that could succeed in delivering him from his mirror-image.

It is thus no longer possible for us to think via hypotheses, even hyperbolic hypotheses. The hypothesis must be a means, but how do means re-enter into the matrix, if not as variables to conjugate with others and with philosophy in particular? Even the void, the catastrophe, disorder, chaos, are means that await a generic end. Where Badiou thinks too absolutely within a philosophical position or Idea, rather than thinking generically and via a matrix, we posit *the fusion of the variables of absolute or philosophical poverty (its Idea or that of Communism) and the radical or immanent poverty of scientific stripping-bare, as unity under-determined by the latter.* Communism, but of

course—there has never been any other solution worthy of
Humans and sought by them; but a generic or non-standard
communism rather than a supposedly "true" authoritarian Idea
of it. If these are the variables, there is no more spontaneous
practice of philosophy that would ceaselessly presuppose itself—
the philosopher as subscriber to the vicious circle—here it is no
more than a "first" means alongside others. We avoid contenting
ourselves with formulas that are too general, and with their
bipolar reversal, "poverty, therefore communism," or formulae
of the military and authoritarian type ("those who have nothing
have only their discipline"). For even the most naked or the
most absurd discipline demands means or weapons—even the
mere human body, which is the a priori form of every weapon,
rather than a weapon to be incorporated or taken in hand. We
shall oppose to Badiou-the-Disciplinary another slogan: *the
only weapon of the poor, stripped not only of all but once and
for all of the All itself, is invention*. It will be a matter of passing
from absolute poverty (the philosophical loss of philosophy) to
radical poverty as non-philosophical loss of philosophy.

Let us pose a last question worthy to attract the mockery of
philosophical opinion: how can we recognize a "poor man," and
what does "pauperized"—or in more statist manner, "undocumented", really mean? For philosophy, it is almost self-evident,
give or take a few definitions: the poor man *is recognized or can
be identified* by subtraction, by the suspension or privation of
certain predicates, but without this touching on the sufficiency
of philosophy, always ready to return because it is in reality
that which assures this recognition, and furnishes the means

for it—just like our favorite philosopher, who distributes his rare truths and, what is more, the proper names that go with them. The true Idea of an "authentic" poor man, as we come to understand, is that of the philosopher himself, who incarnates it as a paradigmatic character: the richest man, not necessarily yet actual or actualized, but endowed with a capital of potentialities that enables him to wait for history to reach its end, or who himself comes to his end. But for the non-philosopher, the poor man is not so easily identifiable, once the sufficiency and authority of these super-predicates of the All and of Position are in turn suspended and processed. From the poor man of philosophy, who always hopes for a minimum of documentation, we must distinguish the radical Stranger—very different, neither with nor without documentation, neither with nor without identity, but who works at transforming, with the aid of the world, the definitions of himself that he has received. What does "undocumented" mean, exactly? It is a matter of a wholly negative subtraction by the philosopher who, himself, can then return with all the positivity of the Good Samaritan. But if this subtraction is radical rather than a vicious circle, it must be without return: no Samaritan comes to the help of the undocumented. Or if a "subject" can come to the aid of the Stranger, it will be the generic subject, that is to say the humans of-the-last-instance rather than the philosopher who, in fact, instead plays the role of the Bad Shepherd.

Let us set out again from the in-One, from superposition as radical immanence. What is the Stranger-subject, the old individual philosophical subject who we might call the

Two-in-One, when it is no longer given in-All, but as relative exteriority of a radical transcendence-in-immanence? On the margin of the One or of immanence, the Two of the Stranger is contributed or announced as unifacial image-(of)-the-One, an image once and for all. The Two cannot reflect the ever-irreflexive One, which would thereby become Two; it is one image each time, not two, then three, four images. Thus the image-(of)-the-One (or, if you like, the individual Stranger as marginal image of the Last Instance) is not a double of the One, or an image in any sense whatsoever. Apart from the State, and what remains of it in Badiou's authoritarian philosophism, no one could recognize the One by intuiting its image—it is an affect of the unique image, and one that prohibits seeing the One itself as separated. Man-in-person or the generic Last Instance is he whose "person" as Stranger prohibits me from recognizing him in himself or from identifying him through given predicates, and who is the object of an obscure or secret praxis that we have called the lived-without-life. Classically, the image is first, but it presupposes the prior-to-priority of the One without giving it one more time. For example, the "One" of philosophy itself is precisely this image that we must relate, or "contribute" as each time unique, to the radical One and not to absolute Being. The radical One is that of a stance, and is given as a lived-without-life or is felt through and through in the image where, however, it is never projected, as in a first image that would precede it. As to this image itself that is the Stranger-subject or, in origin, the old individual ego become marginal, we know that it is of double-aspect, double interpretation, that it is a

Two. The One being this time unifacial, there can be, according to the perspectives of the world, a thousand different images in which it is incarnated as stance, but only one each time—even if this unifacial image is also, ambiguously, as we say elsewhere, the (non-)One (the one and only document of the Stranger), and the non-(One) (his thousand documents), through which we have the sole access possible to the One. The One itself is not an external access to the world, but something immanent that goes or under-goes or that transcends, without itself giving rise to a double transcendence. The One advances incognito before its image, or traverses it.

Notes

Preface

1 [Translator's note—*Planification*: Laruelle intends this word to cover a variety of meanings including: (1) What he will describe as a materialist stratification and quasi-reductionism in Badiou's thought; (2) The distinctions between the *planes* [*plans*] of Being and appearance, and also the various planes of philosophy, meta-philosophy, etc.; (3) An allusion to the four-year *plans* of the communist economies; (4) The modern ideal of planning found in Leibniz, and in capitalism, or in Heidegger's account of modern exploitation; (5) Plato's philosophy as an ordering into planes of anterior knowledges—myth and mysteries, physis, sophistics, the polis. This key term, which I thus preserve as a neologism, brings with it a planned/planar conception of philosophy to which Laruelle will oppose a thinking of waves and fluxes—and of bodies, but not Deleuzian surfaces or the Badiousian planes of an "order-structure" (see A. Badiou, *Second Manifesto For Philosophy*, tr. L. Burchill (Cambridge: Polity, 2011)].

2 A. Badiou, *Logics of Worlds*, tr. A. Toscano (London/NY: Continuum, 2009).

3 F. Laruelle, *Philosophie non-standard* (Paris: Kimé, 2010).

Introduction

1 [Translator's note: Laruelle opposes the "matter" [*matière*] of
philosophical materialism to the "materiel" [*material*—a neologism
in French] which is that of the "lived" [*vécu*]. This is to be
distinguished, at least provisionally, from the "materials" [*matériau*] of
non-philosophy (which include, of course, philosophy).]

2 [Translator's note: *relancer*—to resume, reinitiate, extend or continue,
in the sense that a vector, in physics, can be extended or continued
through addition of another vector.]

3 A. Badiou, *Being and Event*, tr. O. Feltham (New York: Continuum,
2005).

4 A. Badiou, *Manifesto for Philosophy*, tr. N. Madarasz (Albany: SUNY
Press, 1999); A. Badiou, *Second Manifesto For Philosophy*, tr. L.
Burchill (Cambridge: Polity, 2011).

5 T. Aguilar, "Badiou et non-philosophie: un parallele", in
Non-Philosophie, le Collectif, *La non-philosophie des contemporains*
(Paris: Kimé, 1995).

Chapter 1

1 [Translator's note: Not without a certain deadpan humor, Laruelle
articulates his work into (so far) five clearly-delineated stages,
Philosophie I–V, which he characterizes as renewed efforts toward
an identical aim, with each new wave propelled by the force of new
means and resources. In *Philosophie I* (1971–81) Laruelle carried
out his apprenticeship within, and his heretical separation from,
phenomenology, critique and deconstruction. In *Philosophie II*
(1981–95) "non-philosophy" emerged explicitly, and was developed
and reworked throughout *Philosophie III* (1995–2000) and *Philosophie
IV* (2002–7), which, very broadly speaking, direct special attention
to the relation between non-philosophy and, respectively, science
and religion. Laruelle now asserts (see the Preface, above) that
non-philosophy has entered into a new period, *Philosophie V*

(2007–present), characterized by the use of the quantum concepts of superposition and non-commutativity discussed throughout the present work, in which he now speaks of his work as "Non-Standard Philosophy." For a list of works belonging to each period (excluding *Philosophie V*), see the bibliography included in R. Brassier, "Axiomatic Heresy," in *Radical Philosophy* 121 (September–October 2003). See also A. P. Smith, "Thinking From the One: Science and the Ancient Figure of the One," in J. Mullarkey, A. P. Smith (eds), *Laruelle and Non-Philosophy* (Edinburgh: Edinburgh University Press, 2012), 19–41: 27–30]

2   F. Laruelle, *Théorie des Étrangers* (Paris: Kimé, 1998).

3   [Translator's note: Devices of the form *x* (*de*) *y* are used regularly by Laruelle, and should be understood as carrying a multiple meaning: *force* (*de*) *pensée*, as the author indicates here, signifies a "thought-force," to be understood on the model of Marx's "labor-power" [*force de travail*]; but also a "force that belongs to thought," and ultimately the coalescence and the identity (or superposition) of the two terms. A formulation such as *immanence* (*à*) *soi* invites the reader to elide the genitive, and can be read as indicating that "immanence to self" refers ultimately to an identity of "self-immanence." Owing to the syntactical differences between English and French it is difficult to render this ambiguity entirely consistently and preserve the various senses. Different translators of Laruelle's work have opted for different solutions here. We have maintained the *x* (*of*) *y* structure (therefore preserving the allusion to precedents such as Derrida's "force (of) law") but added hyphenation so as to suggest that each such formula should be read as a semantic unit, with the inherent possibility of contracting their three terms into one (hyphenated) term. Unfortunately, in a case such as "force-(of)-thought" this leaves to the reader the translator's task of reversing noun and adjective so as to yield the allusive "thought-force."]

Chapter 2

1   François Laruelle, tr. A. P. Smith (London/NY: Continuum, 2010).

Chapter 6

1 [Translator's note: Laruelle's neologism *en-semblisme* is a "portmanteau" word in which he intends to converge *semblance* ("seeming") and *ensemblisme* ("set-theoreticism") by way of an *en-* ("in-") that refers to immanence by recalling the One-*in*-One. It is thus a kind of (untranslatable) non-philosophical deconstruction of set-theoreticism as mathematical theory.]

2 A. Badiou, *Being and Event*, tr. O. Feltham (New York: Continuum, 2005), 30.

Chapter 7

1 A. Badiou, *Theory of the Subject*, tr. B. Bosteels (New York: Continuum, 2009).

2 [Translator's note: *sous-venue*—to be understood as cognate with "under-determination," "under-going" refers to a becoming that does not take place at the level of representation but at a deeper (quantum) level.]

Chapter 8

1 [Translator's Note: Undocumented—*Sans-Papiers*: lit. "without papers"—those immigrants to France who do not have official permission for their residency or employment in the country—and whose cause Badiou has taken up both politically and philosophically in various works.]

Index